North Yorkshire

A DOG WA   E

Corina Inverno

COUNTRYSIDE BOOKS
NEWBURY BERKSHIRE

First published 2013
© Corina Inverno, 2013
Reprinted 2015, 2017

COUNTRYSIDE BOOKS
3 Catherine Road
Newbury, Berkshire

To view our complete range of books,
please visit us at
www.countrysidebooks.co.uk

ISBN 978 1 84674 303 0

Designed by Peter Davies, Nautilus Design
Produced through The Letterworks Ltd., Reading
Printed by The Holywell Press, Oxford

Cover photograph by Ian Horner

Contents

Walk

Appendix

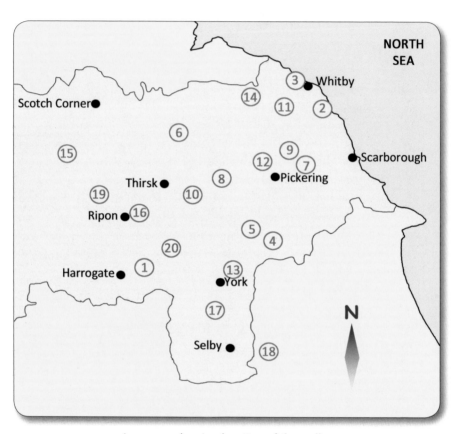

Area map showing location of the walks.

INTRODUCTION

If you love dogs, walking and North Yorkshire then this book is for you. The vast area has endless opportunities for you and your dog to try out many different types of terrain; from ancient paths across heather-clad moors and picturesque dales, to seaside routes and rambles through pretty villages.

The North York Moors are perfect if you and your dog are looking for energetic walks with plenty of steady climbs, great views and peace and quiet. Prehistoric paths along high ridges, sandstone tracks and ancient turf roads all criss-cross the moors offering fascinating routes between villages. It has the largest expanse of heather upland in England, made up of more than 500 square miles of natural beauty including forests, hills and dales.

The Howardian Hills is an Area of Outstanding Natural Beauty; it covers 79 square miles of woods, farmland and historic parkland between the North York Moors and the Vale of York. Walks here can be strenuous, so get yourself and your dog ready for a bit of exercise!

The Yorkshire coastline features beautiful little coves and long sandy beaches for you both to discover. Routes by the sea are great for long runs, swims, or simply to blow the cobwebs away in any season.

Most importantly, North Yorkshire offers you and your well-behaved chum plenty of opportunities for off-the-lead romps or a paddle, or swim. If you cannot rely on your dog to come back when called however, please keep him or her on a lead, and in any case always take heed of signs asking for dogs to be on the lead. All of our walks mention these notices and try to explain why they are there.

My husband Ian and I started walking seriously in the mid-1990s, and three years ago we were joined by our energetic Norfolk Terrier, Izzy. Our rambles take us all over the beautiful and dramatic countryside of North Yorkshire, where we love discovering new dog-friendly walks and places to go for tea and buns (or something a bit more substantial) – so long as they also welcome dogs! A year ago we began documenting the best dog-friendly walks we know, set up a website and also started writing this book.

Most of the walks start in or near towns and villages and all of the cafés and pubs mentioned are dog-friendly, but it's also worth checking with them about opening times and when they will be serving food.

Details of individual maps you should use for each walk are supplied, with the grid reference for the starting point. Although the walks and directions are very detailed, it is always advisable to carry a map, as well as food and drink – for you *and* your dog of course, just in case.

We hope that you enjoy getting out and about on these walks and have lots of fun together.

Corina Inverno

ADVICE FOR DOG WALKERS

Access and livestock

Walking in the North Yorkshire countryside is exhilarating and can be great exercise for you and your dog, while also helping to build and strengthen the bond between you both. Please remember, however, to enjoy the great outdoors responsibly, showing respect for the countryside and those who live and work there – whether they have two legs or four!

You can expect to see sheep and cattle periodically on some of the routes in this book and we always make sure that Izzy, our Norfolk Terrier, is under close control whenever they are encountered. Please observe any signs asking for dogs to be kept under control when walking. You don't have to put your dog on a lead on public paths as long as they are under close control but if you can't rely on your dog to be obedient, then it may be best to keep them on the lead.

Some parts of the North York Moors National Park are home to a number of protected ground-nesting birds and you will see signs asking for dogs to be on a lead in these areas. You may pass through these 'restricted' areas, but must keep strictly to public footpaths and bridleways. Some signs occasionally say 'No Dogs' but these refer to dogs straying off the paths rather than the land being closed to all access. The North York Moors National Park website www.northyorkmoors.org.uk includes a section called 'Walking your dog', where useful information can be found about accessing the area. As ever, you should always clean up after your dog and dispose of it responsibly.

Footwear, mud and ticks

Walking boots and waterproofs – including leggings – are recommended for all of our walks as you will encounter varying terrain, streams and possibly mud. As we all know, the British weather is notoriously changeable so be prepared. For a handful of the walks, for example: *York: with Dick Turpin and Little Nell,* and along the shore from *Sandsend to Whitby*, a sturdy pair of shoes should be just fine.

Remember, where there is livestock there may also be ticks, so it's always worth checking yourself and your dog after each walk to make sure that none have been picked up. You can remove ticks with a tick-remover purchased from a pet supplies shop, or have them removed by a vet.

Stiles and dog-gates

Many of our walks do not include stiles, but those that are encountered often have dog-gates or gaps in adjacent fences or walls, which most dogs can easily pass through. Some walks however, include stiles at which dogs may need a helping hand.

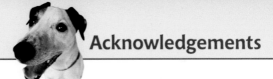
ACKNOWLEDGEMENTS

Thanks to Ian Horner for taking all the pictures, for helping me to write the walks and for his support in the production of this book. Thanks also to Mum and Dad for their help. Special thanks go to Izzy, our Norfolk Terrier, for her help in testing the walks and the dog-friendly places we visited. Big hugs to Jill, John, Bernie and Saffie for starring on the front cover and thanks to all at Countryside Books for putting our favourite walks into print. Final thanks go to all the cafés and pubs who made us feel very welcome.

PUBLISHER'S NOTE

We hope that you obtain considerable enjoyment from this book; great care has been taken in its preparation. Although at the time of publication all routes followed public rights of way or permitted paths, diversion orders can be made and permissions withdrawn.

We cannot, of course, be held responsible for such diversion orders and any inaccuracies in the text which result from these or any other changes to the routes, nor any damage which might result from walkers trespassing on private property. We are anxious though that all details covering the walks are kept up to date and would therefore welcome information from readers which would be relevant to future editions.

The simple sketch maps that accompany the walks in this book are based on notes made by the author whilst checking out the routes on the ground. However, for the benefit of a proper map, we do recommend that you purchase the relevant Ordnance Survey sheet covering your walk. The Ordnance Survey maps are widely available, especially through booksellers and local newsagents.

Knaresborough, the Nidd Gorge and Old Bilton

Between points 3 and 4, follow the yellow waymarker and head towards the trees and the river Nidd.

This is an energetic romp – mostly off-lead, with some hearty climbs and the added bonus of an opportunity for a swim in the quieter parts of the river Nidd. With only three stiles to negotiate – one of which has a dog-gate – the route will please most dogs and their owners. The river flows through the stunning Nidd Gorge from the viaduct at Bilton to just south of Knaresborough, a pretty market town which has many dog-friendly places to pop into for refreshments to round off your day.

The town is famous for the Knaresborough Bed Race, which has been run every summer since 1966. Teams of six, and one passenger, decorate special tube frame 'beds' for a parade through Knaresborough, before competing in a bed-push race.

Terrain

Mostly grassy paths, tarmac lanes and cycle tracks but includes some steep descents and climbs by the river, which may be muddy after wet weather.

Where to park

Conyngham Hall pay-and-display car park in Knaresborough (GR SE345572). **Map:** OS Explorer 289 Leeds.

How to get there

From the A59 Harrogate to York road, turn into the Conyngham Hall pay-and-display car park by the bridge over the river Nidd opposite the World's End pub. By train – Knaresborough station is just five minutes' walk away, along Water Bag Bank and Waterside. By bus – Harrogate and District buses, operated by Transdev, serve Knaresborough.

Nearest refreshments

There are plenty of dog-friendly pubs and cafés in Knaresborough, including Blind Jack's, the Mitre Inn, Marigolds Café and Boating, the Guy Fawkes Arms and the Riverside Café on Waterside.

The Walk

• •

1 Turn right out of the car park and cross the bridge over the river Nidd. Take an immediate right opposite Mother Shipton's Cave and follow the sign for the **Ringway Footpath** and Conyngham Hall Trail. Pass through the gate and head into the park, with the river and car park to the right. Your dog may be let off the lead here. Stay ahead on the cycle track, ignoring the sign for Macintosh Park, and continue on a small bridge over a beck. Follow the waymarked Ringway Path (cycle track) uphill.

2 Keep ahead to a metal kissing-gate next to a cattle grid and continue on the tarmac path, with the tree-line to the right and an open field to the left. Pass

Dog factors

• •

Distance: 7¾ miles.
Road walking: A small amount in Old Bilton village.
Livestock: There may be some cattle on a very short section.
Stiles: Three but all have gaps, which most dogs can pass through.
Nearest vets: Forest House Veterinary Surgery, Knaresborough.

through another metal kissing-gate, with a cattle grid, to an enclosed path bordered by trees to the right and a wire-and-post fence to the left. Cross a quiet road, the entrance to **Bilton Hall**, and continue ahead on the tarmac Ringway Footpath/Beryl Burton Cycle Way, passing a house to the left as the track bears right then left.

❸ At a wooden footpath sign, turn right following the signs for **Ringway Footpath and Knaresborough Round**. Head along the track towards a waymarked gate and stile on the edge of a wooded area. Even large breeds of dog should be able to slip through with no problem. Continue towards a metal gate and just before it, follow the waymarker to the right, keeping a fence to the left and trees to the right. At a fork, take the right-hand path down through the trees towards the river Nidd.

❹ Follow the steps to the riverside, where there will be an opportunity for your dog to have a paddle or a swim, conditions permitting. Continue along the path, with the river to the right. Near a footbridge, keep ahead following the Nidd Gorge footpath sign along duckboards which make the path passable even when the river is high.

❺ The path turns away from the river then back again. Cross a plank footbridge, then a stile next to the river. Again, most dogs will be able to slip under. There is another chance for paddling and swimming here. Cross another stile with a dog gap, towards more duckboards. Keep straight ahead on the path, ignoring another that branches uphill to the left.

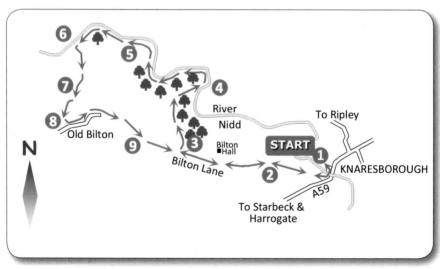

Knaresborough, the Nidd Gorge and Old Bilton ❶

Heading along the path beside the river Nidd.

6 Near to where the buildings of **Scotton Mill** come into view on the other side of the river, follow a flight of wooden steps uphill to the left. At Milner's fork, continue left towards Old Bilton; this is not signposted but just continue heading uphill along the enclosed path. After emerging from the trees, the 'golf balls' of RAF Menwith Hill can be seen in the distance to the right.

7 Follow the path along the edge of a field towards a settlement, keeping the hedge to the left. The path becomes enclosed as it heads downhill, passing farm buildings. Pass through a waymarked gate and follow a public bridleway sign to the left, along the track from Woodside Farm.

8 At the end of the track, turn left onto a quiet road, which passes in front of the Gardener's Arms pub. The road passes through the village of **Old Bilton**. There is a pavement, and there are very few cars here. Continue ahead, passing a caravan park to the left and the Bilton Pet Hotel to the right. The no-through-road becomes a cycle track – the Beryl Burton Way.

9 Keep ahead, passing the track taken earlier towards the Nidd Gorge. At the entrance to Bilton Hall, cross the road and retrace your steps towards Knaresborough to the bridge across the river, and the car park.

2

Robin Hood's Bay

*In the early stages of the walk, making tracks along the old railway line
from Whitby to Scarborough.*

With its wide, easy-to-follow path, this circular walk offers a good steady climb, opening up magnificent views of the North Sea, the coast and Ravenscar. Much of the route allows your dog plenty of freedom, with the opportunity for safe off-lead time. The return path along the cliff tops eventually drops into historic Robin Hood's Bay, with its attractions, pubs and cafés. The beach here is dog-friendly and open all year round.

There is reputed to be a subterranean network of passages linking the houses of Robin Hood's Bay, which was used during the late 18th century when smuggling was rife on the Yorkshire coast.

Robin Hood's Bay

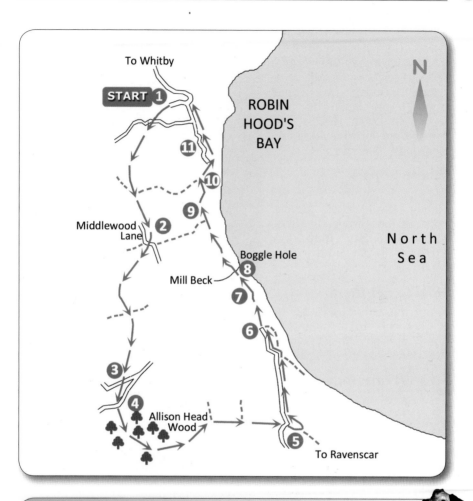

Dog factors

Distance: 6½ miles.
Road walking: A small amount on a very quiet road in the middle of the walk, and through Robin Hood's Bay village at the end.
Livestock: Some sheep and horses possible, but always fenced off from the path.
Stiles: None.
Nearest vets: The Beck Veterinary Practice, High Stakesby, Whitby.

North Yorkshire - A Dog Walker's Guide

Terrain

The outward leg is mainly on the trackbed of the former railway to Scarborough, the return includes two steep climbs using steps. The final section in Robin Hood's Bay can be busy at holiday times or weekends.

Where to park

Pay-and-display car park on Station Road, after turning right at the Grosvenor Hotel (GR NZ948054). **Map:** OS Explorer OL27 North York Moors – Eastern area.

How to get there

From the A171 Whitby to Scarborough road, take the B1447 at High Hawsker, which runs down into the village.

Nearest refreshments

The Laurel Inn allows dogs (☎ 01947 880400) and there are cafés with comfortable outside seating areas.

The Walk

• •

1 From the car park, follow the road to the right, immediately passing the village hall and old railway station buildings. The quiet road is part of the **Cinder Track** – a cycle path on the old railway line from Scarborough to Whitby. It is waymarked as part of the National Cycle Network. The track drops down to cross a road. Turn right for a short way then follow the Cinder Track sign to the left.

2 The route sticks to the old trackbed for the next hour, passing through farmland, and often thickly lined with trees. The track drops down to cross **Middlewood Lane** then back up to continue along the Cinder Track.

The view towards Robin Hood's Bay from the quiet road between the old railway line and the cliff-top path.

③ After passing the former **Fylinghall** station master's house and remnants of the platforms, descend a flight of steps to a quiet road. Cross over and immediately climb some more steps back to the track – the steps can be avoided by staying on the track to the right, down to the road, and crossing there. When the railway was still in use, it was carried over the road here by a bridge.

④ The track continues under a substantial bridge and starts to climb as the tree canopy opens. After passing **Allison Head Wood**, the track bears left to

North Yorkshire - A Dog Walker's Guide

Browside Farm from where there are splendid views of the Yorkshire coastline and the North Sea.

5 After the track bears right, pass under a stone bridge with a brick arch, then turn left onto a short path which leads to a single-track road. With a fine sea view ahead, follow the road as it meanders downhill towards **Stoupebrow Cottage Farm** – keeping your dog under close control. As the road straightens, there are spectacular views of Robin Hood's Bay and its cliffs in front.

6 Continue on past a sign for Ravenscar and at the end of the road by Stoupe Bank Farm, keep to the right following a waymarked path for the Cleveland Way and beach. Head downhill along the stone step path, and cross the footbridge over **Stoupe Beck** to the steps back up the cliff. If the tide is favourable, it is possible to walk back to Robin Hood's Bay along the beach from this beautiful spot.

7 Continue up the steps and follow the cliff-top along a wide, grassy path next to a wooden wire-and-post fence. Behind are great views to Ravenscar with its cliff-top hotel. It may be wise to keep your dog on a lead here due to the erosion of parts of the cliff edges.

8 At a National Trust sign for Boggle Hole, descend some steps to a quiet road and cross over, before heading a short distance to the right. Turn left at a sign for **Boggle Hole** and refreshments, following the path over the footbridge and passing the youth hostel to the left. There is another opportunity to head to the beach at this point. Once across Mill Beck, climb some more steep steps and follow the path up into the trees.

9 Pass through a gate and continue ahead along an enclosed path with fine views of Robin Hood's Bay straight ahead. After passing through the next gate, turn right while remaining on the waymarked coastal path. Again there is some erosion here – so keep your dog under close control.

10 The path leads to a flight of wooden steps; keep descending to the right towards the slipway at Robin Hood's Bay. At the bottom, the walk continues left towards the village but the beach may just be too tempting!

11 On the road by the coastguard station, head uphill along **New Road**. It may be wise to stop for refreshment along the way before tackling the steepest section beyond the Laurel Inn back up towards the starting point. After passing the roundabout and the Victoria Hotel on the right, continue along Station Road to return to the car park.

3

Sandsend to Whitby

The firm sands left by the departing tide leave plenty of space for your dog to play – Izzy just adores it here.

There's nothing like a bracing seaside walk to blow the cobwebs away, be it windy, sunny or raining – we all love it, and so do our dogs! This is a great, long beach for you and your dog to run around on, with opportunities for tea-breaks at the beginning, middle and end. There's the added attraction of walking towards the historic and atmospheric Whitby Abbey, made famous in Bram Stoker's novel *Dracula*. This walk has no stiles and you can be as laid back or as energetic as you like. On reaching the pretty seaside town of Whitby, you will find that it has many dog-friendly pubs and cafés to visit.

The whole beach is open to you and your dog from 1 October to 30 April. However, between 1 May and 30 September, dogs are not allowed on the small section beyond the Sandside Café around where the stream enters the sea. Watch out for the tides. Tide tables are displayed on the side of the Sandside Café, where the walk starts.

North Yorkshire - A Dog Walker's Guide

Dog factors

Distance: 6 miles; almost all beach except for the short tour of Whitby itself.
Livestock: None – just lots of other dogs!
Stiles: None
Nearest vets: The Beck Veterinary Practice, High Stakesby, Whitby.

Terrain

On the seashore and beach, mainly sand with pebbles, the departing tide leaves a wide smooth surface for running and playing on. The beach is accessed via wooden steps from the road. Pavements and roads in Whitby.

Where to park

There is extensive free parking overlooking the sea on Sandsend Road – the main road from Whitby. Alternatively there is a pay-and-display car park at the north end of Sandsend (GR NZ864125). **Map:** OS Explorer OL27 North York Moors – Eastern area.

How to get there

Sandsend is a few miles north of Whitby on the A174 road to Saltburn.

Nearest refreshments

You can sit outside under cover at the Sandside Café. The Hart Inn at Sandsend is also dog-friendly as is the café, Beckett's of Whitby, in Skinner Street.

The Walk

1 From **Sandsend Road** take the steps near the Sandside Café down to the beach and turn right at the bottom – heading towards Whitby Pier in the distance.

2 Walk along the beach for around two miles to the colourful beach huts and the North Beach Café. If it's the peak season – 1 May to 30 September, take the steps off the beach near the huts and continue along the path above the beach into **Whitby**.

3 Alternatively, from October to April, continue along the beach before heading up one of the many flights of steps to Whitby.

4 Pass through the whale-bones on the West Cliff (there is an information board to explain all) and head along the path, which leads to a flight of steps down to the road below. Cross the road and continue along another path, down some more steps to rejoin the road – **Khyber Pass**, for a short distance.

5 With the abbey now in view ahead, there is the option to turn left along the road and head towards the west pier but our walk continues along Pier Road with its seaside attractions.

6 Just before Pier Road bears to the right and becomes Haggersgate, keep left past the Marine Hotel as the pavement follows the harbour entrance.

Dogs and their people of all sizes and ages can't help but love the wide expanses of the beach near Sandsend.

North Yorkshire - A Dog Walker's Guide

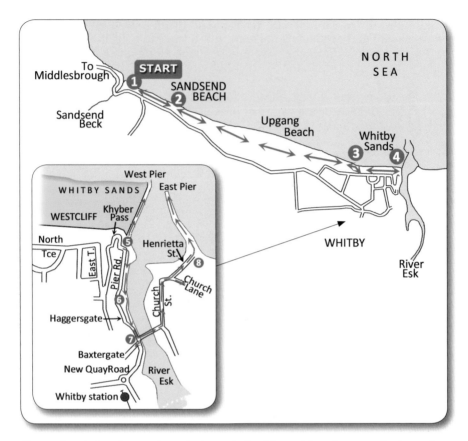

The path rejoins the road on **St Anne's Staith** and heads towards the swing bridge, which opens to allow shipping in and out of the harbour.

7 Cross the bridge over the river Esk then head left along **Church Street** with its Whitby Jet shops and Whitby Jet Heritage Centre. Continue on into **Henrietta Street** which leads to the East Pier with its views of the harbour and the North Sea. Whitby has many attractions which the walker may wish to pursue on different visits according to the time of year, day of the week or prevailing weather. Some walkers may wish to walk into Whitby then spend a few hours in the town before heading back later.

8 To return to Sandsend, first head back to **West Cliff** before accessing the beach, down the steps from the path near the beach huts, depending on the time of year.

4

Westow and the River Derwent

Heading along the lane towards Church Farm Kennels, looking for the waymarker and gate ahead.

This is a very pretty circular walk taking in the river Derwent and Jeffry Bog, a nature reserve where several species of butterfly, moth and dragonfly can be seen. Dogs should be on the lead whilst passing through this area. It is a gentle wander through arable fields, with plenty of wide open spaces and a lovely riverside section; the perfect walk for you and your dog. There are no stiles to negotiate and the route offers great views of the beautiful Yorkshire Wolds through quiet, unspoilt countryside. Westow is situated within the Howardian Hills, an Area of Outstanding Natural Beauty, with panoramic views of the North York Moors National Park to the east, and the Yorkshire Wolds to the south.

Dog factors

Distance: 4¼ miles.
Road walking: A tiny amount right at the start, leaving Westow, and then along a quiet road from the church.
Livestock: Very little – a few cows in one field.
Stiles: None.
Nearest vets: Station House Vets, Welburn.

Terrain

Mostly on flat, green paths through fields, by the riverside or on quiet local roads. The Jeffry Bog plantation can be muddy, but there are duckboards in the worst areas.

Where to park

Roadside parking in Westow village (GR SE754653). **Map:** OS Explorer 300 Howardian Hills & Malton.

Looking back at St Mary's church, Westow, from Church Lane.

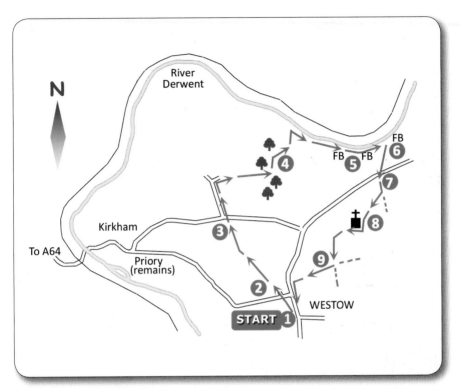

How to get there

Turn off the A64 York to Scarborough road at Whitwell-on-the-Hill, and follow the road downhill, over a level crossing, past Kirkham Priory and on to the next village, Westow.

Nearest refreshments

The Stone Trough Inn near Kirkham Priory is dog-friendly. ☎ 01653 618713.

The Walk

• •

① Start on the main road in Westow by the Blacksmiths Arms. Keeping the pub to the right, head towards the sign for the road to Kirkham and York. At the junction, take this road for a short distance before turning right at the end of the stone wall onto a track heading across the field. There isn't a waymarker, but a weathered road sign, 'Unsuitable for Motors', marks where the track joins the road.

2 Take the track along the edge of the field, keeping a hedge to the left, with the outskirts of the village and the Wolds to the right. After a while the track becomes enclosed by small trees on either side before coming out at a road junction.

3 Cross over and head along the quiet road opposite, following the sign for **Firby**, before turning right at a bridleway sign for the river Derwent (½ mile). Keeping ahead past houses, the road turns into a farm track and continues between two fields. Head towards the tree-line and once past it, turn immediately left along the edge of a field keeping the trees to the left.

4 Where the path bears right, look out for an opening in the trees leading down to a waymarked gate. Pass through the gate into a field and keep ahead towards the river with the railway line beyond it. The path bears right and continues alongside the river, which is now to the left. On entering the next field, an old waymarker on a fence points the way. Keep following the path through the fields by the river, occasionally passing through a waymarked gate. As the name suggests, **Jeffry Bog** can be muddy underfoot but there are duckboards to help in the worst areas and the real pleasure comes from being so close to the river at this point.

5 Cross a footbridge into another field and keep to the path at its lower end by the river. After crossing another footbridge, head towards a wire-and-post fence, where to the left there is a waymarker sign pointing right.

6 Head away from the river, up the bank, keeping the fence to the left, looking for a waymarked kissing-gate in the top right-hand corner of the field. Pass through the gate and continue along an enclosed track to a road.

7 Cross the road and following a public bridleway sign, head up the lane for Church Farm Kennels. Where the lane bears left, follow a waymarker into a field. Ignore the farm gate in front and follow the hedge line, keeping it to the left, and after passing another waymarker, head for a kissing-gate straight ahead, which leads to a small enclosed area and another kissing-gate.

8 Pass through the gates and follow the path around the church, keeping it to the right. Head away from the church along a quiet road with fields and views of the area all around. The road turns left through 90° and heads back towards the village.

9 At a public bridleway sign, follow a path to the right – slightly uphill between two fields. Approaching the village, the path becomes a quiet residential road – there is a dog-waste bin here. Continue along the road, turn left at the end, and head back into **Westow**.

Welburn and Castle Howard

The path through the woods on the return to Welburn, with plenty of space for dogs to run around in.

This walk passes through beautiful woodland and fields, offering inspirational views of the Castle Howard estate and the Howardian Hills, with its pretty villages. The stately home and its monuments act as attractive markers to help navigate your route, and your dog will be pleased that the only stile on this walk has a dog-gate.

Castle Howard is one of the grandest private residences in Britain. Most of it was built between 1699 and 1712 for the 3rd Earl of Carlisle, to a design by Sir John Vanbrugh. The house is surrounded by a large estate which at one time covered 13,000 acres, and included the villages of Welburn, Bulmer, Slingsby, Terrington and Coneysthorpe.

North Yorkshire - A Dog Walker's Guide

Dog factors

Distance: 7 miles.
Road walking: A short distance on a quiet road midway along the route.
Livestock: None, but some animals may be visible, fenced-off in adjacent fields.
Stiles: One, with a dog-gate.
Nearest vets: Station House Vets, Welburn.

Terrain

Mostly on flat, grassy paths along farm tracks and quiet tarmac roads. There is one moderate climb, through a wooded area at the start of the walk.

Where to park

On the roadside in Welburn village (GR SE721681). **Map:** OS Explorer 300 Howardian Hills & Malton.

How to get there

Turn off the A64 York to Malton road at Barton Hill, following the brown signs to Castle Howard. After passing under the monument, turn right at the crossroads following the sign to Welburn.

Nearest refreshments

Leaf and Loaf Artisan Bakery and café, on Main Street in Welburn, is dog-friendly and has a fine selection of foods. ☎ 01653 618352.

The Walk

1. Start on the main road in Welburn near the Crown and Cushion pub. Head along the road with the pub to the left, then turn left down **Water Lane**. At the end of the lane, continue along a track to the left, following a sign for Coneysthorpe. In the spring and summer, dogs need to be on the lead here due to the presence of ground-nesting birds.

2. At a crossing of paths, keep ahead following the public bridleway towards the trees. Pass through a waymarked gate into the woods, following the clear path as it drops to a footbridge ahead on the left. Cross the bridge and continue uphill through the woods – ignoring the wide track that crosses the path. Following the sign to Coneysthorpe, leave the wooded area and

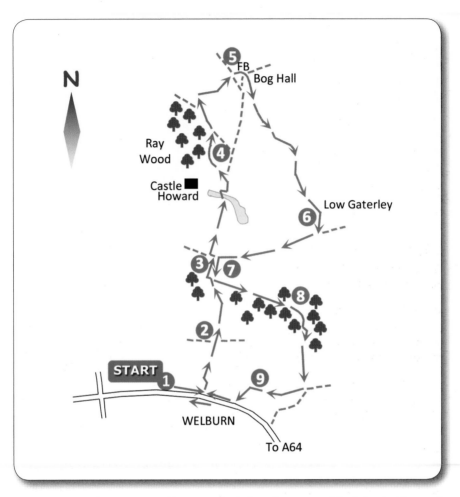

continue ahead to a tarmac lane. To the left is the **Pyramid** of Castle Howard and the stately home.

3 Turn left, then immediately right along a wide grassy path between two fields – still following signs to Coneysthorpe. To the right is the Castle Howard Mausoleum. Cross the bridge over the lake then pass through a kissing-gate. Head up the grassy path diagonally to the left over the brow of the hill in front. There may be cattle in this field, so be prepared to put your dog on the lead here. Pass the **Temple of the Four Winds** before following a stone wall. There are great views of the gently undulating Howardian Hills to the right.

4 At the end of the wall, turn left towards a large white waymarked gate. Pass through the kissing-gate next to it and continue along the path with an old stone wall to the left and a wire-and-post fence to the right. Following a waymarked sign for the **Centenary Way**, turn right onto a farm track.

5 Follow the track across a bridge over **Mill Hills Beck** and continue slightly uphill to a junction of paths near some farm buildings. Following the sign for Gaterley (1 mile), head along a track between the farm buildings following a waymarker. The Mausoleum is again visible as the track continues. Cross the beck again, guided by a sign for the Centenary Way.

6 At **Low Gaterley**, turn right following the Centenary Way and continue to a quiet tarmac road. Turn right following the sign for Welburn. The quiet straight road cuts between two fields and is used by very little traffic. Izzy was not on the lead at this point, but remained under close control. Castle Howard is again visible to the right.

7 Follow a wide path to the left, signposted for Welburn; if it looks familiar, that's because it was used earlier in the walk. Just inside the tree-line, turn left through a gate following the sign to Crambeck onto a wide path through a wooded area – perfect for off-lead romping along this lovely path through the trees.

8 Just before reaching another Castle Howard monument, take the right-hand path following the Centenary Way. The path leads downhill through the woods to a stile with a dog-gate. Cross the stile and continue ahead to a junction of paths by a signpost for Coneysthorpe and Welburn. Take the Welburn path and on leaving the trees, pass through a gate into a field and continue uphill along its left-hand edge. Pass a waymarker post and keep ahead as the path bears right to a public footpath sign to Welburn (½ mile).

The picturesque and tranquil countryside around Castle Howard, with the Mausoleum in view on the right.

⑨ Follow the path towards **Welburn**, with the village coming into view ahead. The clear grassy path passes through a field towards the hedge-line in front. At a crossing of paths, continue ahead following a yellow waymarker, between the hedge and a field. At the end of the hedgerow, follow the waymarker pointing diagonally left across a field. Pass through a gate in the corner of the field, turn right and head back into Welburn.

Osmotherley and the Cleveland Way

The view heading back towards Osmotherley, approaching the gallop at point 7.

This surprising walk with its invigorating climbs and expansive views of the Vale of York, Roseberry Topping and the North Sea, will allow your dog extensive off-lead freedom and a couple of opportunities for a paddle along the way. Much of the route is on the Cleveland Way and the paths are well defined and easy to follow.

The Cleveland Way is a National Trail from Helmsley to Filey. It is 109 miles (176 km) long and takes in the North York Moors National Park, which has one of the the largest expanses of heather upland in the UK.

At 1,049 ft (320 m), Roseberry Topping offers views of Captain Cook's monument at Easby Moor. This distinctive hill, located near Great Ayton, has a half-cone shaped summit with a jagged cliff, and is sometimes compared with the much higher Matterhorn in Switzerland.

Dog factors

Distance: 6 miles.
Road walking: A small amount midway round, with a wide grass verge.
Livestock: None.
Stiles: One, with which dogs may need a helping hand.
Nearest vets: Forrest House Veterinary Group, Northallerton.

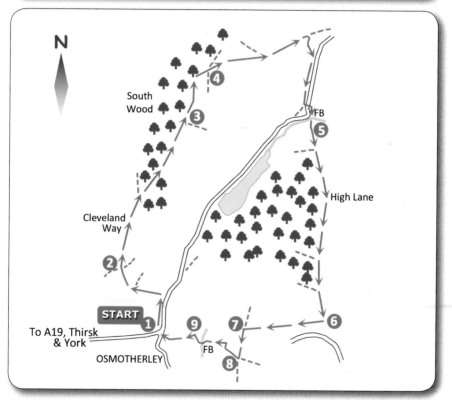

Terrain
Mostly on field paths and across moors.

Where to park
Plenty of street parking in Osmotherley.

North Yorkshire - A Dog Walker's Guide

How to get there
Osmotherley is signposted from the A19 Thirsk to Middlesbrough road and the A684 from Northallerton (GR SE456973). **Map:** OS OL26 North York Moors – Western area.

Nearest refreshments
There are cafés in Osmotherley, and dog-friendly pubs: the Three Tuns, the Golden Lion and the Queen Catherine Hotel.

The Walk

1 Start on the green in the centre of Osmotherley near the obelisk. Following the sign for Cote Ghyll Caravan Park and the youth hostel, head uphill on the pavement alongside North End. Ignore the first public footpath sign on the left and continue out of the village towards the 30 mph road signs. At a Cleveland Way signpost – for Scarth Nick 2½ miles – head left along **Ruebury Lane** passing a dog-waste bin. After passing the driveways to a number of houses, continue ahead slightly uphill while enjoying the grand views of Black Hambleton, Osmotherley and the Vale of York. Continue along the obvious path as it bears right towards a junction of paths near a farm.

2 Keep straight ahead, staying on the **Cleveland Way**, with a hawthorn hedge to the left. After passing through a waymarked kissing-gate, take the right-hand path uphill - still following the Cleveland Way. The wide path climbs steadily into **South Wood**, which, thanks to extensive tree-clearance, is not claustrophobic. As the path climbs higher it becomes more rugged before levelling out at a viewpoint looking across the Vale of York. The path narrows and continues along the high edge of woodland and a drystone wall.

3 Keep ahead through two gates either side of a road running up to a communications station. Continue along the path with a drystone wall to the right, beyond which Roseberry Topping can be seen in the far distance. The path bears right and passes through two waymarked gates in quick succession before coming to a junction of paths.

4 Continue along the Cleveland Way, diagonally across **Scarth Wood Moor** towards the hills. The path undulates downhill, with Roseberry Topping and the North Sea visible in the distance. At a new wooden signpost, turn right following a public bridleway towards a quiet lane which runs to the **Cod Beck Reservoir**. Turn right along the green path next to the road and, as the lane turns sharp right towards the car park, keep ahead towards a footbridge over a beck where your dog may enjoy a paddle.

5 Cross the footbridge and head uphill along the rugged path **(High Lane)**. The path is wide and eroded, with moorland all around. After passing a path to the right, which heads down to the reservoir, continue through, or around, a metal gate. With the edge of a plantation to the right, keep ahead with Black Hambleton visible in front. Ignore two more footpath signs to the right before taking a third just before the track reaches a road.

6 Continue on the wide grassy track with a wire-and-post fence to the right, Black Hambleton to the left and views of the Vale of York straight ahead. Where the track ends, keep going towards a waymarked stile with a dog-gate. Cross the stile and enter the field, keeping ahead on a grassy downhill path with a drystone wall to the left. Continue through a large wooden gate.

Izzy makes a new friend – who isn't going to share his stick with anyone – on the Centenary Way path around Osmotherley.

7 Continue downhill to another wooden gate with the warning 'Caution horses crossing at speed – look left'. Pass through the gate and cross the gallop to another gate on the other side. Pass through the gate and turn left downhill with the gallop now to the left.

8 At a wooden Cleveland Way sign in the hedgerow, turn right through a gap in the wall marked by two tall thin stones. Turn right onto a green track which winds downhill, and just before reaching **Whitehouse Farm**, follow the Cleveland Way sign to the right. After passing a waymarker on a stump, go through two gates as the path drops downhill towards the woods ahead. Cross a track, then head for a footbridge over a beck visible in the trees ahead where there is another pooch paddling opportunity.

9 After crossing the bridge, the path winds steeply up the wooded ridge using a series of steps. At the top, pass through a gap in a wall onto a stone path which becomes enclosed after passing through a kissing-gate. With Osmotherley church in view, keep ahead through another kissing-gate and two narrow gaps to a quiet road. With your dog back on the lead, cross the road and continue on the narrow path between the cottages of Osmotherley, before emerging in the centre of the village opposite the green.

Dalby Forest and the Bridestones

One of the Low Bride Stones along the wide path near point 2.

There is a sense of wild freedom on this route, where your dog can enjoy extensive time off the lead along grassy tracks and paths. In spite of the title, there is little time spent in the actual forest as most of the walk is through peaceful open countryside, with great views of the North York Moors and the 'other-worldly' Bridestones. The Bridestones are knobbly sandstone outcrops formed around 150 million years ago and can be seen along the nature trail in Dalby Forest surrounded by 300 acres of moorland. In addition to our walk, there are many other trails in Dalby Forest for you and your dog to explore.

Terrain
Mostly on easy-to-follow tracks and green paths, with an uphill climb at the start.

Where to park
Low Staindale (Bridestones) car park (GR SE879905). **Map:** OS Explorer OL27 North York Moors – Eastern area.

How to get there; access and approaches information
The Bridestones are best reached by using the Dalby Forest Drive, a toll road, out of **Thortondale**. When entering Thornton-le-Dale from Pickering, take the first left turn (signposted to Dalby Forest Drive and to Whitby). After about a mile take a right turn onto a minor road that leads via the toll road to Low Dalby. Continue along the scenic Dalby Forest Drive, passing many parking and picnic areas, to the car park at Low Staindale. If you get as far as the hairpin bend by Staindale Lake, turn back, you have just passed it! *Dalby Forest Toll, cars: March to October, £7 all day or £4 after 4 pm, November to February, £4 all day. The Forest Drive is open from 7.30 am to 8.30 pm. (Accurate at date of publication.)*

Nearest refreshments
The nearest dog-friendly pub is the excellent Fox and Rabbit just south of Lockton on the A169 Whitby road, near Dalby Forest. ☎ 01751 460213. The café at the Dalby Forest Visitor Centre does not permit dogs but Dalby Courtyard café has outside seating where you and your dog can sit in warmer weather.

The Walk

1 Take the footpath from the car park and head towards the trees, passing a National Trust sign for the Bridestones. Continue ahead on the path and at a kissing-gate, bear right to a fork by a National Trust information board. Take the left path and walk uphill, bearing right near the top of the climb through an area of birch trees, heading for the open moorland.

Dog factors
Distance: 4½ miles.
Road walking: One short section towards the end of the walk.
Livestock: There may be cattle around the farm in Point 5.
Stiles: Two. Larger dogs may need help.
Nearest vets: Edgemoor Veterinary Practice, Pickering.

2 Continue on towards the impressive **Low Bride Stones**, now in sight ahead. From here there are great views of Bridestone Griff below and the North York Moors. Having passed the stones, there is the option of a quick detour to the left to view the **High Bride Stones**. The walk, however, continues to the right, following a yellow waymarker along a narrow path through heather on **Bridestones Moor**, making for the tree-line in front.

3 The path comes out onto a broad track. Turn left and follow the track along the edge of a forest for about ½ mile. This is a great area for your dog to romp around.

4 At a National Trust information board by a gate, turn left along an uneven path and, keeping the wire-and-post fence to the right, head towards a pond. The path wiggles downhill and stays close to the fence. At a National Trust marker-post, bear right towards a waymarked stile. There is no dog-gate here. Smaller dogs will probably be able to squeeze under but larger ones will have to jump or be carried over.

5 Turn left immediately through a metal gate leading to an enclosed farm track with wide grass verges on either side. This is another great opportunity for some bounding about. Approaching some farm buildings, turn right following a yellow waymarker into a field, with the hedge and fence to the left. Look out for cattle at this point. At the corner of the fence, follow another waymarker to the left on a grassy path along the edge of a bank which slopes away to the right.

6 With a wire-and-post fence to the left, head towards the tree-line in front while looking for a stile at the bottom right-hand side of this rectangular enclosure. Cross the stile into the next field – again there is no dog-gate. Keep straight ahead along the edge of the field respecting the landowner's request to 'use the grass verge' with the fence and drystone wall on the right. Bear left, staying on the edge of the field, with buildings in view ahead and continue towards a wooden gate.

Dalby Forest and the Bridestones

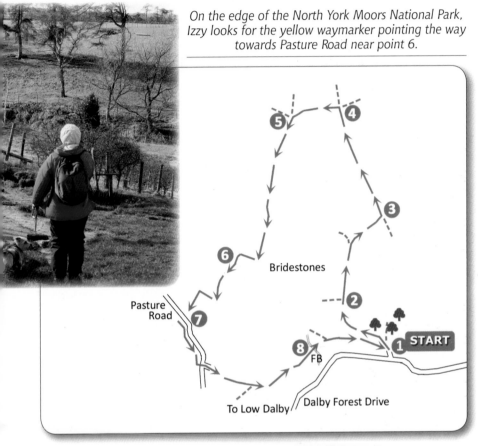

On the edge of the North York Moors National Park, Izzy looks for the yellow waymarker pointing the way towards Pasture Road near point 6.

7 Pass through the gate and turn left along the single-track **Pasture Road** for a short distance. After the road dips and bears right, follow a green and white footpath sign to the left along a wide enclosed farm track. Keep ahead through the farm towards a metal gate by a National Trust 'Bridestones' sign. Follow the track downhill through another gate towards a house. It is safe for well-behaved dogs to be off the lead again here.

8 Bear right past the front of the house and turn immediately left. After passing chicken coops behind the house, the path becomes a grassy track as it heads downhill towards a stream. Use the stepping stones and continue ahead, with trees and a wire-and-post fence on the left, towards a kissing-gate. Pass through the gate and head back along the path to the car park.

Helmsley to Rievaulx Abbey

About to continue on the Cleveland Way.

There are plenty of off-lead opportunities for well-behaved dogs on this easy-to-follow route to the tranquil Rievaulx Abbey as well as great views of Helmsley Castle, the pretty Hambleton Hills, and the remote Rye Dale. With no stiles to negotiate, and dog-friendly refreshment stops available in the charming market town of Helmsley, and at the abbey, this walk will not disappoint.

Helmsley Walled Garden, Helmsley Castle and Rievaulx Abbey permit dogs as long as they are on a lead. The magnificent Rievaulx was one of the earliest Cistercian abbeys in England. Both the abbey and the castle are managed by English Heritage.

Helmsley to Rievaulx Abbey 8

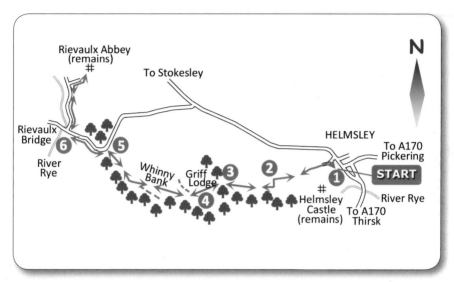

Terrain

The path is clear and easy to follow and, apart from a couple of energetic climbs, is flat for most of the way round. There is a little road walking on the approach to Rievaulx Abbey.

Where to park

The Cleveland Way pay-and-display car park in Helmsley, just off Church Street/B1257 (GR SE611839). **Map:** OS Explorer OL26 North York Moors – Western area.

How to get there

Helmsley is on the A170, roughly halfway between Thirsk and Pickering, and within easy reach of York using the B1257.

Dog factors
. . . .
Distance: 5 miles.
Road walking: Approaching the abbey – along a quiet road.
Livestock: Sheep may be in the first couple of fields near the start of the walk.
Stiles: None
Nearest vets: Edgemoor Veterinary Practice, Helmsley.

Nearest refreshments

Porter's, on Bridge Street in Helmsley, permits dogs inside at the back of the café, or outside in the quiet seating area away from the road. ☎ 01439 771555. Rievaulx Abbey permits dogs on a lead and there is a seating area outside for a tea and buns stop.

The Walk

1 At the entrance to the car park, and with the toilet block to the right, look for a sign for the Cleveland Way and Rievaulx (2½ miles). Follow the wide track with stone walls on either side and, after passing a sign for the Helmsley Walled Garden, go through a kissing-gate into the field ahead. There may sheep in this field, and a sign requests that dogs be kept on a lead. Continue along the edge of the field through another kissing-gate while heading uphill. Don't forget to turn round to enjoy the view of Helmsley Castle behind.

2 At the next kissing-gate, turn immediately left to a pathway, enclosed by the hedge to the left and a wire-and-post fence to the right. Well-behaved dogs can be set free again. Follow a waymarker arrow right and continue along the enclosed path at the edge of fields. At a waymarker post, follow the sign for the Cleveland Way and Rievaulx Abbey to the left, then head downhill into the wooded area. Continue down, and then up, some steep stone steps – a bit of a challenge for small dogs perhaps but Izzy really enjoyed them and bounded up with no problem.

3 At the top the view opens up as the route passes a Cleveland Way sign and then another yellow arrow. Keep ahead on the wide, stony path, with fields to the right and woodland to the left. After passing another waymarker, there is a seat by a sign for the Cleveland Way pointing back to Helmsley. To the right is a stone gatehouse, **Griff Lodge**.

4 Continue ahead, crossing the track from the lodge and bear right, following another Cleveland Way sign as the wide and grassy path once again heads for the trees. Continue downhill as the path bears left and keep ahead, ignoring tracks to the left and right.

5 At a road, after ensuring your dog is on the lead, turn left initially along an elevated footpath. Once round the right-hand bend, the path joins the quiet road.

Rievaulx Abbey

6 After a short distance, turn right at **Rievaulx Bridge** and continue along the narrow road to the abbey. Dogs are permitted on a lead in the abbey grounds and gift shop. They are not allowed in the café but there is plenty of outside seating, with a perfect view of the abbey. Exuding peace and tranquillity, the magnificent Rievaulx Abbey lies in a remote wooded dale by the river Rye, sheltered by hills. It was among the first Cistercian abbeys to be created in England and became one of the wealthiest until it was dissolved by Henry VIII in 1538. Rievaulx is now one of the most complete and atmospheric of England's abbey ruins. Once refreshed and ready, head back down the road and retrace the outward route back to Helmsley along the Cleveland Way.

Levisham and Newton Dale

Heading up the track by Dundale Griff, Izzy spots the moors ahead.

This is a great walk in any season, using a pleasant mix of relatively sheltered parts of the moor, with a couple of moderate climbs and some very dramatic views. Your dog will enjoy some off-lead time and perhaps a paddle in Levisham Beck, but if there are sheep about on the moorland, please keep him or her on a lead.

Levisham station is the first halt after Pickering on the North Yorkshire Moors Railway. It was opened in 1836 by the Whitby and Pickering Railway before being taken over by the York and North Midland Railway nine years later. Originally worked by horses, the line saw its first steam-hauled service from Pickering in 1846.

The line became part of the nationalised British Railways in 1948, but the Beeching Report of 1963 recommended the closure of all railways serving Whitby, and the line from Malton via Levisham was closed in 1965. After the line was taken over by the NYMR in 1973 however, Levisham station was reopened and it is once again possible to reach Whitby on a steam-hauled train.

Dog factors
••

Distance: 5½ miles.
Road walking: A small amount on the very quiet roads around Levisham.
Livestock: Sheep on the moors.
Stiles: One
Nearest vets: Edgemoor Veterinary Practice, Pickering.

Terrain
Grassy paths across moorland or through wooded areas. There is one steep climb, but the views are well worth the effort.

Where to park
Roadside parking in Levisham village (GR SE834906). **Map:** OS Explorer OL27 North York Moors – Eastern area.

How to get there
From the A169 Pickering to Whitby road, turn west around 5 miles north of Pickering, following signs passing through Lockton to Levisham.

Nearest refreshments
Horseshoe Inn at Levisham and the Fox and Rabbit Inn (10 minutes away on the A169) are both dog-friendly and serve food.

The Walk
•••

❶ With the Horseshoe pub behind, head south along the main street of the village. There are wide grass verges for you and your dog to walk on. Where the road bends right, downhill, look for a wooden footpath sign on the left. Follow the path downhill as it hugs the hotel boundary hedge, keeping close to the tree-line as it goes. Ignore the path that heads straight down into the valley bottom.

❷ The path is clear and easy to follow, and levels out before climbing a flight of wooden steps. Continue along the gently undulating path, high above the valley below. At a wooden signpost, continue ahead towards Horcum.

❸ After a while **Levisham Brow** can be seen below on the right. Continuing onwards, the view opens up to reveal the moors and valleys. A gnarled wooden footpath sign points back towards Levisham; not to be followed though. The path heads downhill to a waymarked gate. Pass through it and continue to a footpath sign near **Levisham Beck**. In this area there are plenty of opportunities for romping, paddling and swimming, or simply having a break.

4 At a sign for Dundale Pond turn left uphill on the broad green path as it becomes narrower and more eroded, with another beck to the right. At the end of the tree-line, keep right where the path forks, heading towards a wooden signpost. There may be sheep grazing here as the walk enters moorland.

5 Following the sign for Levisham station, keep straight ahead passing **Dundale Pond** to the right.

There are options following points 4 and 5 to shorten the walk by heading straight back to Levisham. After passing **Dundale Griff**, follow signs back to Levisham along Limpsey Gate Lane. Or from Dundale Pond, follow the signs back to Levisham along Braygate Lane. Both routes re-enter the village at the Horseshoe Inn.

For the full route, at the corner of a stone wall, continue ahead following a blue arrow, with the wall to the left. Keep straight ahead at the end of the wall to the top of the rise from where there are panoramic views of Newton Dale and the road to Levisham station below.

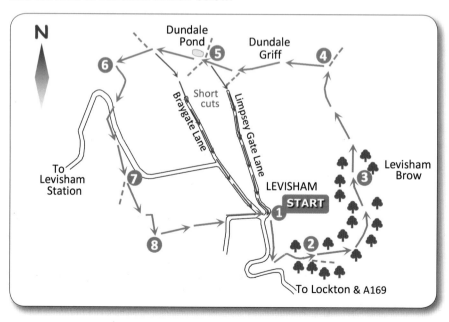

On the wide green path above Levisham station, heading towards point 7.

6 The path heads left downhill towards the road. Turn left at the road and continue uphill for a short distance before following a bridleway sign to a green path above a track on the right. Be careful not to follow the track, which leads to a closed gate and private land. Keep ahead on the green path and look out for a well-camouflaged sign on the right pointing towards Levisham.

7 Take the left fork and follow the path as it climbs quite steeply, but the reward is a wooden seat at the top commanding spectacular views of the moors and Newton Dale. Levisham station is down below, and steam trains can often be seen – and heard! Continuing on, the path bends left and right before leading uphill to a stile.

8 Climb the stile, then turn left immediately along the edge of an arable field, keeping a stone wall to the left. Pass through a waymarked gate and continue ahead to a road. Follow the road straight on for a short distance back into **Levisham**.

White Horse and Kilburn Woods

The White Horse, from the Mouseman visitor centre.

This spectacular little walk with its short, sharp ascent is one to get the blood pumping. Once the steps to the White Horse have been climbed, you will be rewarded, all along the ridge, with superb views of the Vale of York. The return route passes through some pretty woods, well worth exploring from the main path.

The White Horse is a figure cut into the hillside of Sutton Bank, and was created by removing top soil to reveal the limestone underneath. The horse covers about 1.6 acres, and, on a clear day, can be seen from Leeds. A stone sign in the car park reads, 'The Kilburn White Horse. This figure was cut in 1857 on the initiative of Thomas Taylor, a native of Kilburn. In 1925 a restoration fund was subscribed by the readers of the Yorkshire Post and the residue of £100 was invested to provide for the triennial grooming of the figure.'

Dog factors

· ·

Distance: 2 miles
Road walking: None
Livestock: None
Stiles: None
Nearest vets: Skeldale Veterinary Centre, Thirsk.

Terrain

Steep steps, with a hand rail, but after the initial climb, the paths are wide and flat along the ridge then downhill on the way back to the car park.

Where to park

Free car parking at the foot of the steps to the White Horse (GR SE514812). **Map:** OS Explorer OL26 North York Moors – Western area.

How to get there

From the A19 York to Thirsk road, follow signs east to Kilburn village then the brown signs directly to the White Horse car park.

Nearest refreshments

None on the route, but there are refreshments available in Kilburn. The charming 'T' café at the Mouseman Visitor Centre has a comfortable covered, heated outside area where you and your dog can enjoy a break. The Foresters Arms in the village is also dog-friendly.

The Walk

· ·

1 From the car park, follow a sign for the **White Horse Bank Walk** at the bottom of the stone steps. Head up the steps, some are quite steep but there

Heading downhill through the sunlit woods on the way back towards the car park.

is a handrail for assistance. There are great views behind you across the Vale of York as the White Horse comes into view to the left.

2 At the top of the steps, pause and turn left to look down on the top edge of the White Horse, while enjoying the panoramic views to the west. Continue on the path along the ridge, keeping the White Horse and a roped fence to the left. Most dogs will be fine off the lead but beware the runway belonging to the gliding club. It may be advisable to keep your dog under close control or on a lead here, especially when the winch is despatching gliders into the sky.

3 On reaching the glider information sign to the right, a red waymarked post points the way along a path to the left, heading downhill into the trees. Head down the rocky eroded path with a fence to the right and trees to the left. The path levels as it passes through a wooded area.

4 Keep ahead all the way to return to the car park where there is a large grassy picnic area with tables and seats.

Grosmont and the North Yorkshire Moors Railway

A former Southern Railway 'Schools' class steam locomotive begins its journey from Grosmont to Pickering along the North Yorkshire Moors Railway.

If you are a fan of steam railways then the start and finish of this walk will be a real treat. The North Yorkshire Moors Railway station in Grosmont welcomes dogs in the outside section of the café and you can even take your dog for a train ride if you like. This is a pretty walk, setting out along the original trackbed, before continuing through woods and out onto the edge of the moors. Your dog is free to be off-lead most of the time.

The route traces part of the original Whitby to Pickering railway, built by George Stephenson and opened in 1836 as a horse-drawn tramway. After being sold to George Hudson, the so-called 'Railway King' in 1845, the line was upgraded to use steam locomotives before being superseded by what is now the NYMR twenty years later.

North Yorkshire - A Dog Walker's Guide

Dog factors

Distance: 4½ miles.
Road walking: A little in the Beck Hole area.
Livestock: Expect to see sheep and maybe cows. Please respect the signs asking for dogs to be on a lead.
Stiles: A few on the way back. Dogs will need to be helped over the one stile that doesn't have a dog-gate.
Nearest vets: The Beck Veterinary Practice, High Stakesby, Whitby.

Terrain
Mainly on good, wide paths, but it can get muddy towards the end of the walk. There is one steep climb on the road out of Beck Hole.

Where to park
Grosmont Station, or follow the road under the railway to the North York Moors National Park car park on the right (GR NZ828054). Both are pay-and-display. **Map**: OS Explorer OL27 North York Moors – Eastern area.

How to get there
Grosmont is 7 miles south-west of Whitby and is signposted from the A169 Whitby to Pickering and A171 Whitby to Middlesbrough roads.

Nearest refreshments
At the Grosmont station café, as well as the Station Tavern by the level crossing. Dogs are allowed in the station 'tea garden' and can also travel on the trains. There is a small but charming pub in Beck Hole called the Birch Hall Inn. See their website for opening times or call ☎ 01947 896245.

The Walk

1 From the station café, go over the railway line at the level crossing and take a path in front of some cottages on the right. Cross the suspension bridge over the Murk Esk and follow the '**Goathland Rail Trail**'. Go left at the fork and head uphill towards a church. Keeping the church to the left, continue towards a kissing-gate, with a sign pointing towards the Rail Trail. Your dog could now be let off the lead as you go right and continue uphill with Grosmont NYMR locomotive depot visible through the trees to the left.

2 Immediately ahead there is a sign for the Rail Trail. Follow the path to the

left and continue downhill through two gates to a cinder path alongside the railway line, where parked locomotives may be seen. Turn right and follow the path – the bed of the original railway – towards the pretty settlement of **Esk Valley.**

3 At the line of railway cottages, continue on the old trackbed, through the gate into a wooded area. The path is wide and quite flat, suitable for wheelchair users and pushchairs, as well as allowing a good romp for dogs.

4 Keep following the obvious path through gates and over a wooden footbridge, with the NYMR visible to the left climbing through the trees. On the right is the **Murk Esk** again. Your dog may enjoy a quick paddle when the path eventually closes in to run alongside the river.

5 At the next footbridge, stay on the same side of the Murk Esk leaving the 'accessible' path, and taking a more rugged route uphill. Ignore the sign for Egton and keep ahead to an unsigned but obvious route through the trees, before coming to a wall on the right with a clear view of fields. The path rises to a gate, beyond which is the road into **Beck Hole**, so make sure your dog is on the lead before entering the pretty village – a pleasant spot for tea and sandwiches on the green perhaps.

Many of the stiles encountered throughout North Yorkshire are easily navigated by most dogs, as Izzy demonstrates on the way back to Grosmont.

6 Immediately to the left of the gate, the road climbs steeply as it bends sharply right and then left before crossing the railway – a good place to watch the steam trains go by. After the bridge, turn left and continue up the road for a short while towards a farm on the left, where a pathway joins the road from the moor to the right. After passing the farm buildings, there is a waymarked gate to the left. Follow the path through the fields which may have sheep grazing in them, until reaching a farm. Walk through the farm and turn left onto a lane.

7 At the end of the lane, look for a green and white bridleway sign to the right. Take this path through a gate and then another waymarked gate onto a grassy path towards a track lined with hawthorn hedges – dogs are usually fine off-lead here.

N

GROSMONT

To Sleights

START

Esk Valley

Green End

The Murk Esk

Beck Hole

8 Continue downhill to a gate and a sign saying 'Bridleway Closed'. Turn off the bridleway here, at a yellow arrow indicating a footpath to Grosmont down towards the trees on the right. Follow the rugged, obvious path through woodland to a stile with a dog-gate. Continue onwards to the right, to another stile with a dog-gate, before emerging onto the edge of a meadow where you should take the obvious path to the left.

9 Ahead is a double stile – your dog may need help here – and the path continues into the next meadow. Continue downhill towards a footbridge and enter woodlands again. Keep ahead as the path climbs into the trees towards a gate on the right. Pass through the gate and turn left, keeping the tree-line to the left, until you reach a track coming down the hill from the right.

10 Join the track and pass through a gate. Follow a footpath sign downhill along the wide lane. Traffic does occasionally use this lane so keep your dog under control. At the sign for a ford, take the footpath indicated to the left and cross a footbridge over the **Murk Esk**, before climbing a flight of stone steps back to the church by the railway at **Grosmont**. Follow the path through the churchyard and return to Grosmont station.

The Cropton Round

Heading along the bridleway towards point 4, with the Vale of Pickering in view on the left.

This walk offers panoramic views of the Vale of Pickering and the moors, as it meanders in and out of woodland and through meadows along green paths. If your dog enjoys a paddle, there are opportunities along the way for a quick dip. This is a fairly gentle walk with no stiles and just one steep climb at the end, before returning to Cropton's dog-friendly pub for some well-deserved refreshments.

The small village of Cropton is well known for its brewing activities, which date from 1613 when such enterprises were actually illegal. Brewing returned to the village in 1984, when the Cropton Brewery was established. Nearby is Cropton Forest, a mainly coniferous woodland with plenty of great walking and cycling routes just waiting to be explored.

Dog factors

Distance: 5 miles.
Road walking: A tiny amount right at the start, near the pub.
Livestock: Expect to see some sheep. Please respect the signs asking for dogs to be on a lead.
Stiles: None
Nearest vets: Edgemoor Veterinary Practice, Pickering.

Terrain

Mostly on wooded, sheltered paths with some open areas. There is one steep climb at the end but otherwise the walk is mostly on level ground.

Where to park

There is plenty of street-parking in Cropton (GR SE755889). **Map:** OS Explorer OL27 North York Moors – Eastern area.

How to get there

Cropton is north-west of Pickering and is signposted from the A170 Scarborough to Thirsk road.

Nearest refreshments

The New Inn at Cropton marks the start and finish of the walk and is dog-friendly. ☎ 01751 417330.

Heading across the meadow towards Cropton Banks Wood, just after point 2.

The Walk

1 From the New Inn, walk a short distance on the grass verge by the side of the road heading towards Pickering, to a public bridleway on the right by the entrance to the village. Head along the track – your dog may be let off the lead now – and continue straight ahead as it narrows, with hedges on either side. Ignoring footpaths to the left and right, continue along **Bull Ing Lane** until you reach a junction of paths.

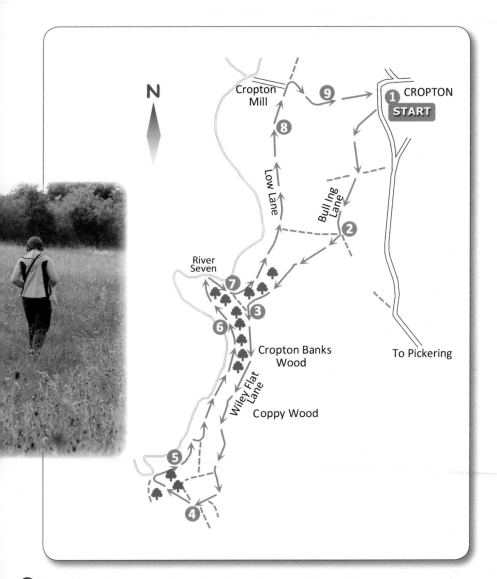

N

Cropton
Mill

CROPTON
START

Low Lane

Bull Ing Lane

River
Seven

Cropton Banks
Wood

To Pickering

Wiley Flat Lane

Coppy Wood

2 Pass through the gate immediately in front and bear right across a meadow heading towards the trees. At the end of the tree-line, pass a waymarker on an old gate post and turn left along the edge of a field keeping the hedgerow to the left, while enjoying views of the moors to the right. Continue through a gate into the wooded area and keep to the high path in line with the tops of the trees below. Keep ahead through a small dip, regaining height immediately, with the hedge on the left. Pass through another gate and keep ahead, ignoring a downhill path to your right.

3 At a fork in the path take either route – they soon re-join – and keep straight ahead, following a blue waymarker arrow attached to a sawn-off tree. Emerging from the wooded area to a view of the rolling hills, ignore a short path and gate to the right, and continue onwards, keeping a wire fence to your left at the edge of a field. The path bears right onto a track from where there are views of the Vale of Pickering.

4 Carry on along the track for a short distance, then leave the bridleway at a junction indicator, following a narrow path down towards the trees. Once in the wooded area, the path is clear and wide as it leads slightly downhill. Ignoring the path to the right, continue on to a signed junction of paths and turn right to follow another track, with a beck visible below on the left.

5 As the track leads into a field, keep towards the left of two gaps in the trees ahead. Turn right uphill through a gate then immediately left, heading for a gate leading into the trees. Follow the path through the woodlands, keeping the beck on your left and ignoring the path joining steeply from the right. If your dog fancies a paddle, there are ample opportunities for a quick dip.

6 Pass to the right of a gate and along a narrow overgrown path while keeping the field to the left. Ignoring the path to the right, go through a rickety gate and continue a short distance towards another gate, to a small meadow with a white cottage in front. Keep ahead to a stone trough and turn right up the track, back towards another gate into the trees.

7 Continue uphill and at a fork, take the left path which widens as it heads downhill through the trees to a waymarked gate. Pass through the gate to a narrower path and another gate by a junction of paths. Ignoring options to Appleton Le Moors and Sinnington, continue ahead towards Cropton, following **Low Lane**, a wide track leading uphill. Where the track bends to the right, keep left along the path and continue ahead.

8 Just before a track from **Cropton Mill** joins from the left, look out for and take a right turn through a gate and continue on the steep path uphill towards the right-hand end of the tree-line. Look for some steps to a little kissing-gate, almost hidden in the corner of the field by a hawthorn tree.

9 Go through the gate and follow the obvious path across the fields, passing a campsite to the left. The path joins a lane back to the road and the New Inn.

York: with Dick Turpin and Little Nell

Izzy trying out the 'going' at the Knavesmire, York's horse racing venue.

The first part of this walk takes you to York's Knavesmire, where your dog can romp around freely on this vast flat, green open space. It is also a very sociable place, with plenty of other dogs to rub noses with. York's famous racecourse is at the Knavesmire, and its inner tarmac path is ideal for a circuit of the course, especially when the grass is wet. The second part of the walk takes in the spookily good bits of historic York, where legend has it the highwayman Dick Turpin used to walk with his dog, Little Nell.

The Knavesmire was York's public hanging place for many years, with gallows being erected in 1379. Dick Turpin, probably the most infamous person to be executed there, was hanged in 1739. It is said that the highwayman and his dog had many adventures in and around York. This walk attempts to give you a glimpse of the old York that Dick and Little Nell might have inhabited.

North Yorkshire - A Dog Walker's Guide

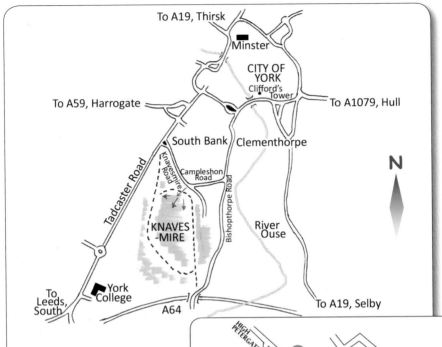

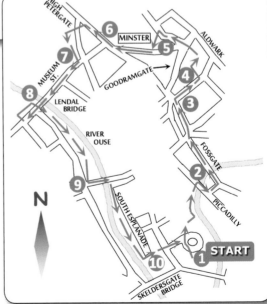

Terrain

Flat, expansive grassed area, with paved internal perimeter road at the Knavesmire; pavements in York city centre.

Where to park

Plenty of free roadside parking on Knavesmire Road, or behind the main grandstands on Racecourse Road (take care to avoid race days). There are various parking options in York, including a large pay-and-display car park at Clifford's Tower – just off Tower Street.

Dog factors

Distance: 2 miles.
Road walking: The entire walk – apart from the Knavesmire – is in York city centre, mostly on pavements.
Livestock: None
Stiles: None
Nearest vets: The Minster Veterinary Practice, York.

How to get there

The Knavesmire is on the south side of York, on Knavesmire Road, just off Tadcaster Road (A64 Leeds). Alternatively, take Bishopthorpe Road from the city and turn right onto Campleshon Road, which leads to the Knavesmire (GR SE596500). **Map:** OS Explorer OL27 North York Moors – Eastern area. The best way to get from the Knavesmire to Clifford's Tower, by car or on foot, is to first head uphill along Campleshon Road then turn left onto Bishopthorpe Road. Continue on towards the centre of York, following the one-way system through Bishopthorpe, Nunnery Lane and Price's Lane onto Bishopgate Street, crossing the river Ouse by way of Skeldergate Bridge. After crossing the river, turn left onto Tower Street then just after passing Clifford's Tower, turn right into Castlegate car park opposite the Hilton Hotel.

Nearest refreshments

Dog-friendly places in the centre of York include the Three Legged Mare on High Petergate, and the Last Drop Inn on Colliergate.

The Walk

Dick and Little Nell used to start their walks in the early evening at Clifford's Tower. Nearby is the Castle Museum, where Dick Turpin was held prisoner before he was hanged at the Tyburn gallows on the Knavesmire.

1 From the foot of the steps to **Clifford's Tower,** head towards the line of trees at the far side of the car park, to a riverside footpath. Take the path, which passes the edge of the **Coppergate** shopping centre and after a short while emerge on to **Piccadilly** where it crosses the river **Foss**. Just over the road here, is the Merchant Adventurers' Hall. Many of the wives of these unsuspecting merchants were robbed by Dick and Little Nell, which is why dogs are not allowed in the gardens here!

Exploring Dick Turpin's York, Izzy passes St William's College near the Minster.

2 Turn right away from the city centre, then left at the roundabout and continue past the cycle racks and bus stops of **Merchantgate** before turning left up the cobbles of **Fossgate**. Follow Dick and Nell's route as it crosses the river again, before continuing up the narrow street. At the end of the road, continue ahead to York's shortest street with the longest name – **Whip Ma Whop Ma Gate**. At the end of the street (blink and you'll miss it!) keep ahead onto **Colliergate**.

3 Where Colliergate bears left, the **Last Drop Inn** is on the right. The original pub on this site would have welcomed shady characters like Dick and Little Nell. Today you and your dog are most welcome in this lovely traditional pub. Ironically, for Dick Turpin, its name is a reference to hanging!

4 After leaving the Last Drop, turn right out of the door then right into the charming and quiet area of **Aldwark**. Turn left at a sign for Bartle Garth and follow the road with the **Minster** ahead, as it bears right then left to a snickleway on the left, near a sign for Bedern. Follow the narrow passageway, leading to the ancient street of **Goodramgate**. Turn left towards York Minster, then immediately right, to the black and white buildings of **St William's College**. Head past the college with the Minster in front then turn left at Minster Yard, keeping the cathedral to the right.

5 Straight ahead across the road is a Roman column, where it is said the ghost of a centurion walks. With the statue of the Roman Emperor Constantine the Great to the right, continue to the west face of York Minster by the Dean Court Hotel. Turn right along **High Petergate** to another of Dick and Little Nell's favourite watering holes, the **Three Legged Mare** – known to locals as the Wonky Donkey. This friendly pub not only allows dogs, but also offers treats and water too.

6 Suitably refreshed, Dick would have turned left out of the Three Legged Mare, but if you didn't go in, keep ahead on High Petergate towards **Bootham Bar** – the north-western gate of Eboracum, the Roman name for York. To the left across Exhibition Square is York Art Gallery, where there is a dog-friendly summertime pavement café by the attractive water fountains. Cross the road and turn left onto St Leonard's Place.

7 At the traffic lights, turn right onto **Museum Street** and after passing York Explore library to the right, head across **Lendal Bridge**. Turn right at the end of the bridge along a short section of the city walls to a flight of steps on the right, down to the river.

8 At the bottom, pass under Lendal Bridge onto **Wellington Row**. After a short while, pass through a gate in the wall to the riverside path and walk by the river Ouse before climbing up the steps towards **Ouse Bridge**.

9 At the top of the steps, cross the road, then head across the bridge. At the end of the bridge, drop down a flight of stone steps to the **Kings Staith** alongside the river. This ancient area has long been a popular place for refreshments and Dick and Nell would probably have finished their evenings off with a night-cap here, before heading home – said to be one of the houses on South Esplanade, which is ahead on the left. Continue alongside the river, with the blue-painted Skeldergate Bridge in front.

10 At the end of **South Esplanade** turn left, and walk with the parkland to the right, back towards **Clifford's Tower**. Should you or your dog want a longer walk, continue on the riverside path towards Fulford as far as you both need.

Danby, Ainthorpe and Little Fryup Dale

Heading down from Ainthorpe Rigg.

This walk offers a real taste of the North York Moors, revealing some of its prettiest dales and valleys without the need for endless trekking across moorland – not always such fun for your dog! There are some lovely enclosed paths where your dog will enjoy romping off-lead, as well as a couple of moderate climbs to get the blood pumping. The route offers panoramic views of the moors and dales, giving a feeling of wide open space and freedom that's not found everywhere.

When people first settled in Danby Rigg, about 8,000 years ago, the area was covered by woodland. Early farmers burned it away to grow crops and keep cattle, and the height of the Rigg was useful for early warning of impending attack. The woodland eventually died out due to cattle grazing, creating the moorland that can be seen today.

Dog factors
· ·

Distance: 6 miles.
Road walking: More than on most walks, but the roads are quiet and the views at the end are well worth it.
Livestock: Expect to see some sheep on the moors and respect the signs asking for dogs to be on the lead.
Stiles: Three, larger dogs may need some help.
Nearest vets: Wilton House Veterinary Clinic, Guisborough.

Terrain
Mostly on green, enclosed or rugged moorland paths, with a couple of gentle climbs and one fairly steep descent.

Where to park
The pay-and-display car park at the North York Moors Visitor Centre (GR NZ718084). **Map:** OS Explorer OL 27 North York Moors – Eastern area.

How to get there
From the A19 York to Thirsk road, take the A172 towards Stokesley. Avoiding the town centre, continue on the A173 for a short distance before turning off to follow the signs towards Kildale. Keep on the same road through Castleton towards Danby and once in the village follow the brown sign for the North York Moors (NYM) Visitor Centre. From the A171 Whitby to Middlesbrough road, near its junction with the B1366 (Liverton Road), follow the sign to Danby and then from the village continue to the NYM Visitor Centre.

Nearest refreshments
The Fox and Hounds Inn at Ainthorpe is dog-friendly, and there is plenty of outside seating in the gardens at the North York Moors Visitor Centre.

The Walk
· ·

1 From the car park at the North York Moors Visitor Centre, cross the road following the footpath sign to Ainthorpe and pass through a gate with a yellow arrow and a fish symbol (Esk Valley walk). Head along the grassy path towards the trees ahead, then follow the yellow arrow past a statue of an 'old man' over a footbridge towards another gate. Continue on the path at the edge of a field as it bears slightly right and uphill towards the railway – **the Esk Valley line**. After obeying the warning signs, cross the line and continue ahead along

Just after crossing the railway line, pass through the gate and follow the sign towards Ainthorpe.

the wide, grassy path. At the corner of the field, pass through a gate and turn right along a quiet road, following the footpath sign to Ainthorpe.

2 Just after the road bends, look for a green and white public footpath sign on

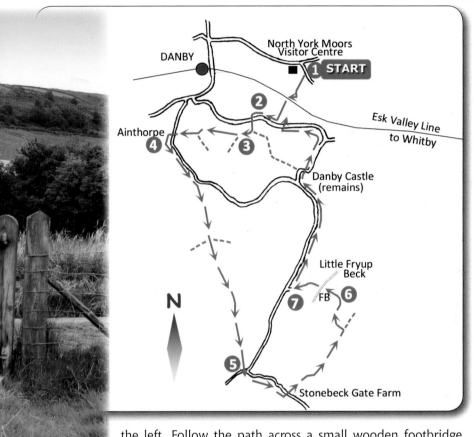

the left. Follow the path across a small wooden footbridge and pass through a gate. The path is obvious as it heads along the side of a field next to a hawthorn hedge. The views are lovely now and in late summer, the famous moorland purple heather will be coming through. Follow the path as it turns to the right and follow the yellow waymarker on an old stile ahead, keeping the hawthorn hedge to the left.

❸ Continue ahead at the next waymarked stile – most dogs will be able to slip through it – and keep a stone wall to the right. Cross another stile – some dogs will appreciate a helping hand over this one – and head along the enclosed path next to a drystone wall on the left. At the next stile – again, some dogs will need help here – cross over and turn right onto a stony enclosed track towards the village of **Ainthorpe**.

④ At the road, turn left uphill past the dog-friendly Fox and Hounds Inn. Stay on the road as it leaves the village but, where it bears left, follow the bridleway sign on the right pointing towards a path through a large waymarked gate on the edge of the moor. The path continues across **Ainthorpe Rigg** which is rugged in parts and offers beautiful views of the surrounding countryside. There may be sheep or ground-nesting birds around so be prepared to put your dog on the lead. The path climbs steadily and is easy to follow as it passes occasional blue waymarkers and tall stones, which act as guides when the weather is not so good. At a junction of paths keep straight ahead and drop down into **Little Fryup Dale**. Before doing so, don't forget to take a breather to enjoy the views.

⑤ The initially rugged path descends sharply but soon turns grassy as it heads towards a road junction by a farm. There is a pleasant green area here with a bench – perfect for a tea and buns stop. Suitably refreshed, head along the road opposite the path from the Rigg and continue downhill with a drystone wall on the left. After passing through a gate next to a cattle grid, look for a bridleway sign on the right pointing down a track to the left. Head down the track, following the sign for Stonebeck Gate Farm and Forester's Lodge. Visible on the left is Ainthorpe Rigg, and the path down from the moor. Keep on the track as it bears left towards **Forester's Lodge** – following the yellow waymarker. Just before reaching the farmhouse turn right and follow another waymarker through a gate into a field.

⑥ Bear left towards the corner of the farm buildings, then head diagonally and downhill towards a wooden gate in a stone wall with a faded waymarker. Follow a succession of waymarkers as the path heads along the edge of the field next to a fence and then bears left, downhill towards a gate and some trees. Pass through the waymarked gate, cross a footbridge over **Little Fryup Beck** and continue along the clear track, enclosed by walls on each side – ideal conditions for well-behaved dogs to be allowed off-lead.

⑦ Pass through a large gate and continue on the track as it winds uphill towards a road – time for the lead again. Turn right along the road **(Castle Lane)** and continue past Crossley Gate Farm towards the remains of **Danby Castle**. The views along this section are very pretty and the road is quiet. Near the castle, turn right at the junction and continue along the road downhill towards the 14th-century packhorse bridge – **Duck Bridge** – by a ford across the river Esk. Continue on past the bridge, heading once again for Ainthorpe but just before entering the village, turn right through a gate into a field and follow the grassy path back towards the railway. Again, after taking heed of the warning signs, cross the railway with care and head back along the path towards the North York Moors Visitor Centre.

Entering the village of Wensley, on the way back to Leyburn.

With gentle climbs and stunning views around Wensleydale, this walk is a real gem. Paths meander through a blend of arable and cattle fields, offering you and your dog some healthy exercise amidst the beauty and freedom of the Dales. Views from the Shawl, overlooking Wensleydale, can only be described as magnificent, and the traditional Dales market town of Leyburn is bustling with tea shops and attractions, including the Wensleydale Railway, a scenic heritage line running from Leeming Bar through Bedale and Leyburn to Redmire.

Leyburn Shawl is a bold limestone terrace extending almost unbroken for nearly two miles and gradually rising to a height of 870 ft above sea level. The limestone at this point is around 60 ft thick, forming a very attractive and prominent escarpment overlooking the valley.

Dog factors

Distance: 7½ miles.

Road walking: A short section near the village of Wensley.

Livestock: Expect to see some sheep, and respect the signs asking for dogs to be on the lead.

Stiles: Several. Some dogs may need help but most stiles have dog-gates or something similar.

Nearest vets: Yoredale Vets, Harmby Road, Leyburn.

Terrain

This is a varied walk mostly along clear paths and tracks through fields.

Where to park

Market Square in Leyburn town centre near the Golden Lion and Black Swan hotels – no fixed charge but there is a donation box (suggested contribution £1). If busy, there is a pay-and-display car park nearby, signposted from Market Square (GR SE113904). **Map:** OS Explorer OL30 Yorkshire Dales – Northern & Central areas.

How to get there

From Richmond, take the A6108 to Leyburn. Alternatively from the A1, take the A684 Northallerton to Kendal road through Wensleydale.

Nearest refreshments

There are café options in Leyburn, as well as dog-friendly pubs: the Golden Lion, the Black Swan and the Sandpiper, as well as the Three Horseshoes in Wensley.

The Walk

1 From the car park head across High Street and along Commercial Square towards the Dalesman's Club straight ahead. Keeping the club to the left,

*Striding out along the Leyburn Shawl at the start of the walk
in beautiful Wensleydale.*

head along **Shawl Terrace** following a sign on the side of a house pointing the way to the Shawl. After passing a line of stone cottages, follow another sign for the Shawl and playing fields to the left, then right through a metal kissing-gate. Keep ahead on the stone path through a wooden gate onto the **Shawl**, and immediately take in the view of Wensleydale to the left.

2 After passing the Leyburn Shawl information board, continue ahead along a wide green path passing a children's play area to the right. Once beyond the play area, well-behaved dogs can be let off the lead. Pass through a waymarked gate and keep ahead along the edge of the ridge with a wire-and-post fence to the left and a drystone wall to the right. Continue ahead through obvious gaps in the wall towards the Leyburn Shawl Plantation.

3 Keep a watchful eye out for sheep – especially in the lambing season. The path keeps ahead along the edge of fields, and narrows to a gap in the wall next to a wooden gate. Taking the gap or gate, continue ahead along the path through another almost identical gap and gate before making for another gap and gate near a pretty stone house.

4 Continue ahead, along the elevated path with a drystone wall to the right. There are several benches in this area on which to sit and enjoy the views. The path climbs steadily as it bears to the right following the ridge, with expansive views opening up towards the west.

5 At a fork next to a large gap in the drystone wall, head left downhill alongside another wall towards a waymarked gate and makeshift stile which small dogs will need a hand getting over. Enter the field and follow the path continuing downhill, diagonally across it towards the wall and tree-line to the left. Look for a waymarked metal gate in the corner of the field, leading to a wide farm track.

6 With a drystone wall to the left and arable fields to the right, continue along the farm track towards some farm buildings. The path drops as it passes a cattle shed to the left.

7 With an unfinished stone barn with a corrugated roof ahead, turn left following a waymarker down a farm track. As the track bears left, continue straight ahead, while keeping a drystone wall to the right. Head downhill, passing through a wide gap in the wall onto an enclosed path near waterfalls. Continue past a ruined mill as the path loops round to a quiet road. Cross the road and follow a wooden public footpath sign through a gate and across a short field towards a stile ahead. Cross the stile, which small dogs can go under, and then continue over the Wensleydale railway to another stile with a gate on the other side of the track.

8 Continue ahead along a clear grassy path crossing a field towards a

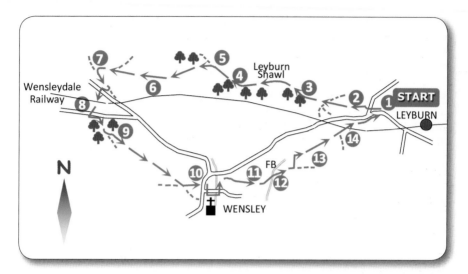

waymarked gate leading to a road. Cross the road and turn left along it, looking for a footpath sign. Turn right at the wooden sign, and head through a gap in the drystone wall along a clear path through the trees. Turn right, then quickly left along a wide clear track following a green and white footpath sign towards a cattle grid. Keep following the track round the edge of the tree-line but at the next cattle grid take an immediate left following the faded waymarker arrow through a wooden gate. Do not cross the cattle grid. Head around the drystone wall looking for a yellow waymarker and a little wooden gate at the edge of a field.

9 Pass through the gate and head downhill alongside a wire-and-post fence next to a horse gallop towards another gate by a footpath sign, pointing diagonally across the next field. Enter this field and aim for a big oak tree, low down to the left. The path crosses a small ladder stile – which most dogs will go straight through – before passing to the left of the oak tree and heading towards a wide metal gate in the corner of the field. Pass through the gate, cross the gallop and turn left along a quiet tarmac track. Keep going until it reaches a cattle grid, where there is also a gate and a dog-waste bin. After passing through the gate, the track, which is actually the access road to the nearby Bolton Hall, enters the village of **Wensley**.

10 Cross the main road through the village, and turn right towards the church. Turn left for a short distance along a road signed for Middleham and Masham, with the church to the right. After the road crosses Wensley Brook, follow a yellow waymarker to the left up a quiet lane, passing a white house to the right. Just after the lane bears right and then left uphill, look for a footpath sign by a gate on the right. Pass through the gate into a field in front of a house, then through another waymarked gate into the next field and follow the line of telegraph poles.

(11) At the far end of the field, pass through a waymarked stile next to a metal gate – small dogs will need a hand here – to a wooden kissing-gate beyond. Enter the next field, and follow the wire-and-post fence alongside the hedge on the right. After passing to the right of a tree, bear diagonally left across the field and head uphill towards a waymarked kissing-gate. Pass through a gate and keep ahead on the path, before turning right through a waymarked gate leading into the **Old Glebe Nature Reserve**.

(12) Cross a small wooden footbridge over a beck and immediately turn left, keeping the drystone wall to the left while heading towards a yellow waymarker ahead. At the waymarker, pass through a narrow gap between two stones and carry on across the field towards a stile ahead. People will have to climb over this waymarked stile but most dogs will probably dive straight under it. Head left across this narrow field towards a tree. After passing the tree, turn right by a wall next to a sports field and cross a small stile – there is plenty of room for all dogs to go around this one. Now keeping the drystone wall to the left, make for a new stile, by a tree, next to a metal gate ahead.

(13) Cross the stile – small dogs will need some help – and head across the next field to another waymarked stile – most dogs will go straight under this one. Continue past a farm on a green path along the edge of a field, sometimes used by horses, towards a gap in the drystone wall and hedge. Keep walking along the left-hand edge of the next field towards a waymarked stile (with a dog-gate), next to a metal gate. Cross the stile and keep to the grassy path along the left-hand edge of the field while heading for a yellow waymarker, by a gap between two pieces of stone. High up on the left is the Leyburn Shawl where the walk began. Continue across this field following a wire-and-post fence, ignoring the track leading away to the left, towards a waymarker on the fence ahead beyond an old stone barn.

(14) Climb another stile, with a dog-gate. Cross the field and pass through a gated gap in the next fence, which leads to the railway line. Cross the railway using the concrete steps over the two fences. The steps are easy, even for small dogs. Continue through the next field, heading diagonally uphill towards a gate and the road, near some houses. Pass through the gate and turn right onto a path alongside but separated from the road. Follow the path back into the centre of **Leyburn.**

Ripon and Studley Royal Park

There are plenty of opportunities for a swim or a paddle on this walk, as Izzy demonstrates.

This circular walk from the centre of Ripon is ideal if your dog likes a good paddle or a swim, as there are many opportunities to get wet in the river Skell along the way. There are no stiles and the enclosed paths provide opportunities for safe off-lead romping. The tranquil Studley Royal Park with its beautiful water garden is a pleasure to meander through, and you can enjoy panoramic views of Ripon Cathedral and the city.

The water garden at Studley Royal dates from 1718 and is one of the best surviving examples of a Georgian water garden in England. The ornamental lakes, canals, temples and cascades provide additional interest in this picturesque area. The medieval deer park is home to 500 deer and many species of plants.

North Yorkshire - A Dog Walker's Guide

Dog factors

Distance: 7 miles.
Road walking: In Ripon, and a quiet section towards the end of the walk.
Livestock: There may be deer grazing in Studley Royal Park, especially from June to August.
Stiles: None
Nearest vets: Bishopton Veterinary Group, Ripon.

Terrain
Mostly on grass or gravel, easily navigable, flat paths.

Where to park
Any of the pay-and-display car parks in Ripon (GR SE314712). **Map:** OS Explorer 299 Ripon & Boroughbridge.

How to get there
Ripon is on the A61 between Harrogate and the A1(M) near Thirsk. Alternatively, leave the A1(M) further south at junction 48 and take the B6265 Boroughbridge Road past the racecourse and into the city.

Nearest refreshments
Various pubs and cafés in Ripon, including the One Eyed Rat and the Water Rat.

The Walk

1 From the main entrance to **Ripon Cathedral** in the centre of the city, walk down **Bedern Bank** and turn left at the roundabout. Head over the bridge crossing the river Skell, then take an immediate left down a flight of steps to the concrete path on the river bank. Turn left and head along the path under the bridge. Continue along the path to the road at **Bondgate Bridge**. Cross the road and make for the gap on the other side to continue on the path with the river once again to the right.

2 At the next bridge, cross **Williamson Drive** and head along the pavement opposite – Barefoot Lane. After a short while, pass through the gap in the stone wall near a dog-waste bin and follow the path under the next bridge, close to the river. With a children's play area ahead, turn left towards some

steps back up to the road, then continue along the pavement for a short distance to **Borrage Green Lane** on the right.

If the river is high, another option is to stay on Barefoot Lane then continue at the bridge straight ahead along Harrogate Road before turning onto Borrage Green Lane.

3 Turn right onto the lane and continue ahead, soon passing another dog-waste bin. As the path becomes greener, the river is re-joined once again through the trees to the right. Weather permitting there are definite paddling and swimming opportunities here.

4 Cross the river at a waymarked footbridge and head along a concrete path at the edge of a park, now with the river on the left. There is another dog-waste bin here. Climb a flight of concrete steps and turn left, and then continue along the pavement following a line of trees on the left, and passing a weir. At the roundabout, turn left following the sign to Fountains Abbey, before crossing the road straight away to use the pavement on the other side.

5 Near the entrance to a caravan park, the road bends to the right. At this point, look for a public footpath sign for Studley Roger and Fountains Abbey on the other side of the road. Cross the road and pass through the kissing-gate onto a path enclosed on each side by hedges. At the crossing of paths keep straight ahead. This enclosed route is easy to navigate and safe for well-behaved dogs

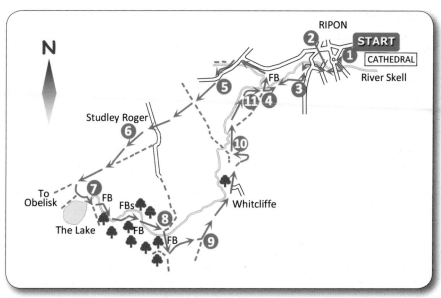

to be let off the lead. After passing through a wooden kissing-gate, the path passes some houses before reaching a road in **Studley Roger** village. Cross the road and head between two more houses along an inclined lane following a public footpath sign. After a short while, the now flat gravel path becomes bordered on each side by wire-and-post fences as it heads towards a tall wooden gate with a hook-lock.

6 Pass through the gate, taking heed of any warning signs about the fawning season for deer (June to August) and ensuring dogs are on short leads as appropriate. Head diagonally left along the grassy path before joining the tree-lined lane heading towards an obelisk. With the monument straight in front, head along the lane then turn left towards the lakeside car park. With the lake in Studley Royal Park coming into view through the trees, bear left onto a path towards its left-hand edge.

7 Cross the wooden footbridge next to a weir and follow the path round before taking the left fork towards a stone footbridge. There are plenty of paddling opportunities on this section as the path continually crosses the stream using stone footbridges. Keep to the path as it follows the stream and eventually head through a metal gate in a stone wall to leave the park.

8 Look out for a waymarked footbridge, approached by a few concrete steps on the right. Cross the stream one last time and head into the trees, following the path round to the right and passing a ford to the left. At a junction of paths take a sharp left, following a blue waymarker. After a short while follow another waymarker through a wooden gate out of the trees and into a field. Follow the grassy path as it bears left with a line of trees through the field.

9 At the end of the field, pass through a gate and turn left onto a lane following a blue waymarker. Follow the quiet lane past **Whitcliffe Hall Farm** and Whitcliffe Grange Livery, enjoying panoramic views along the way, including Ripon Cathedral and the city. At the end of the lane (where there is another dog-waste bin), cross over the road and turn left along the pavement at the edge of a residential area. After a short while, cross back over the road and head along a lane near a sign for **Hell Wath Grove** (don't go right), passing some football pitches on the right.

10 Ahead is a waymarked wooden gate with a dog-waste bin. Do not pass through the gate, instead turn right and head along a path through the trees. Continue ahead on the path through a field, where the river **Skell** on the left can be heard, and stay ahead at the next fork keeping the trees to the left. Follow the path as it heads up a flight of wooden steps before dropping down to the river again using some concrete steps – once again paddling and swimming opportunities here are plentiful.

11 When the fun is over, continue along the riverside past the footbridge crossed earlier in the walk. Head back along **Borrage Green Lane** and the riverside paths to the start by the entrance to **Ripon Cathedral**.

At the beginning of the walk, Izzy takes a keen interest in the river Skell from the path under the bridge.

Acaster Malbis and the River Ouse

Navigating a stile by the river Ouse at Naburn – Izzy went straight under the fence.

This circular walk begins by the banks of the river Ouse in the village of Acaster Malbis, just outside York. Your dog can happily enjoy off-lead time on the wide green paths by the river and even take a swim if conditions permit. Although close to the city of York, this walk, which also takes in arable fields and a disused railway line, gives a real sense of open space and a feeling of being out in the countryside.

The village of Acaster Malbis is popular with visitors and boating enthusiasts and many vessels are moored there throughout the year.

Boat traffic on the river Ouse near Naburn Marina, with the old railway swing-bridge in the background.

Dog factors

Distance: 4 miles.
Road walking: A small amount at the start and end.
Livestock: There may be some cattle on a very short section in Point 3.
Stiles: A few but mostly next to gates which most dogs will be able to pass through or under.
Nearest vets: The Minster Veterinary Practice, York.

Terrain

Mostly on wide, flat paths by the river or on the old railway line. There is just one brief climb – up to the railway which is now used as a footpath and cycle path.

Where to park

Limited parking in Acaster Malbis. Alternatively, patrons can use the car park at the dog-friendly Ship Inn (GR SE590455). **Map:** OS Explorer 290 York.

How to get there

From York city centre, head south towards Bishopthorpe on Bishopthorpe Road. From the racecourse on Tadcaster Road, turn left at York College along Sim Balk Lane. Once in Bishopthorpe, follow the signs for Acaster Malbis.

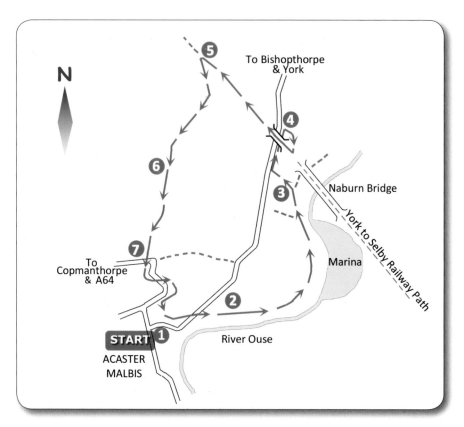

From the A64, turn off at Copmanthorpe, and head through the village following the signs for Acaster Malbis. Once in the village, look for the signs to the riverside Ship Inn.

Nearest refreshments

The Ship Inn at Acaster Malbis stands at the start/finish of the walk and is dog-friendly. ☎ 01904 703888.

The Walk

. . . .

1 From the Ship Inn, head along **York Road**, with a caravan park to the left and the river Ouse to the right. After a short while cross the road and follow a wooden footpath sign up Jorvik Lane towards the river. There is a dog-waste bin under the sign.

② The lane is quiet, only being used by boat owners to gain access to the moorings, so well-behaved dogs may be let off the lead here. On the other side of the river is the village of **Naburn** and the sloped bank offers a doggie paddling or swimming opportunity. The path becomes grassier after passing a stile next to a metal gate – easily passed under by all dogs. Keep ahead by the river bank, ignoring the path as it bends to the left. Instead climb the waymarked stile – there is a big space for dogs to pass through – and continue towards the old **Naburn swing-bridge** in view ahead.

③ Before reaching the bridge, turn left at a waymarked stile by a metal gate. Climb the stile – most dogs will go under the gate – and head in a straight line across the field. Sometimes cattle graze here so be ready with the lead, just in case. At the far side of the field, climb a stile next to a wooden gate – again most dogs will go under it – and turn right, along the road.

④ After a short distance, pass under the bridge then immediately turn right up some steps and head for the **York to Selby railway path** – part of the national cycle network (route 65) and Trans Pennine Trail. There is a dog-waste bin here. Turn to the right and head up a flight of stone steps to the trackbed of the old York to Selby railway line. Turn right at the top and head along the flat, concrete path. This section can be busy but there is ample room for joggers, cyclists, walkers and dogs.

⑤ With the houses of Bishopthorpe visible to the right, turn left along a footpath signposted to Acaster Malbis. Follow the path along the edge of a field with a line of trees to the right and another tree-line in front. Where the tree-line ends, continue ahead between two fields towards the hedge. Cross a stile – it has a big gap for dogs – and continue straight ahead on the path along the edge of a field with a hedge to the right.

⑥ The paths here are grassy and well defined, giving a sense of freedom and of being in the open space, even though the city of York is so near. Cross another stile, with a gap for dogs and continue ahead between two fields towards houses and trees ahead. Approaching a large metal gate with a 'private' sign, bear right towards a tree where there is another stile and dog gap. Keep ahead on the path next to a wire-and-post fence, before crossing a waymarked wooden footbridge to the right, leading to an enclosed footpath.

⑦ Continue along the path to the road and turn left back towards **Acaster Malbis**. Follow the road as it bends to the right, left, then right again before taking a footpath to the left through a caravan park, signposted to Hauling Lane, underneath a sign for Poplar Farm. Head through the caravan park and emerge back on the road near the Ship Inn.

North from Howden

Heading along the wide, grassy path near Park Farm.

This is a great romp through wide open spaces that lets you and your dog enjoy a real sense of freedom and tranquillity. It's a relatively level route along green paths and arable fields, where your dog can be off-lead for most of the time. The bustling market town of Howden and its historic Minster can be seen from the walk. The terrain is largely flat and in some places marshland, much of which is divided by drainage dykes, which are used as markers and guides along the walk. Howden's impressive Minster is well worth a visit. Construction began in 1228, but it was not completed until the 15th century.

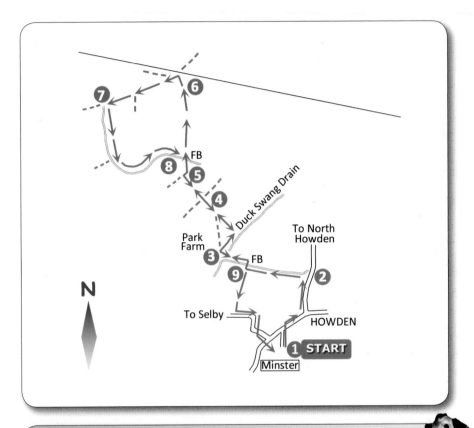

Dog factors

Distance: 6½ miles.
Road walking: A small amount leaving and returning to Howden.
Livestock: None
Stiles: None
Nearest vets: End Cottage Veterinary Clinic, Howden.

Terrain
Mostly on flat green paths, through or alongside fields.

Where to park
Street parking and car parks in Howden (GR SE749283). **Map:** OS Explorer 291 Goole and Gilberdyke.

North Yorkshire - A Dog Walker's Guide

How to get there

Howden is on the A63 from Selby to Hull and is close to junction 37 of the M62, accessed via the A614.

Nearest refreshments

Minster View Hotel in Howden allows dogs in the bar. ☎ 01430 432450.

The Walk

• •

❶ Start at the war memorial in Howden and head along Market Place, passing the White Horse Inn before turning right at the end of the road into **Bridgegate**. After passing the white stone Press Association building, turn left along a road signposted for the Oaks Golf Club & Spa and Bubwith. Continue ahead along a wide pedestrian path, passing some new-build houses to the left.

❷ Just before the 40 mph signs, turn left down a track which leads to a path next to a dyke. The path is partly enclosed by trees and is flat and easy to follow. Ignore a path to the right over the dyke and bear left past a waymarker post for the Howden 20 trail. The path crosses a tiny plank footbridge as the views begin to open up. Where the path meets another, cross a footbridge following the Howden 20 sign and then turn left before continuing ahead towards a farm, with the dyke to the left and fields to the right.

❸ Just after the path crosses another dyke, turn right and walk alongside this dyke, keeping it to the right. After a short while, turn 90° left

Howden Minster.

at a waymarker post and make for another marker post just inside a gap in the hawthorn hedge ahead. Alternatively, after initially crossing the dyke, take a diagonal right path towards the gap in the hedge.

④ Keep following the Howden 20 signs along the wide, green path. With a field and the farm buildings seen earlier to the left, and a hawthorn hedge to the right, continue ahead towards the tree-line. Where the path crosses a farm track, continue ahead on the path towards the trees, following a broken footpath sign tied to a stone bollard.

⑤ On reaching the trees near a junction of paths, follow the Howden 20 sign to the right of a wooden gate and to the left of a metal gate towards an enclosed footpath. During the ground-nesting season, dogs should be kept on a lead in this area. Follow the waymarker to the right then turn left over a wooden footbridge into an open field. Continue straight ahead, following a clear path along the edge of the field to a wooden footpath sign next to the railway line at a level crossing. At this point the Howden 20 route crosses the railway line.

⑥ Turn left and head along the wide, green farm track that runs up to the level crossing – with the cooling towers of Drax power station visible straight ahead in the distance. By a raised mound of land, bear right onto a grassier path and head in the direction of a farm.

⑦ At an old waymarker post near the end of a dyke, turn left and walk alongside the dyke, keeping it to the right. Then follow the tree-line along the edge of the field, passing a red and white gas pipeline marker to the right. Soon after, turn left along a green path cut into the field towards another old marker post in front of the trees. Continue on the path as it heads back towards the footbridge crossed earlier.

⑧ After re-crossing the footbridge, head along the enclosed path, once again on the Howden 20 trail, making sure dogs are on leads in the ground-nesting bird area. Having returned to the junction of paths, retrace the outward route back towards Howden and continue straight ahead along the track. Howden Minster is visible in the distance ahead. After passing the farm buildings – to the right this time – continue to the dyke and turn right, then left, back to the footbridge crossed earlier in the walk.

⑨ Cross the bridge then continue straight ahead along a wide, green path by the **Howden Marsh Nature Reserve** towards some houses and trees. At a footpath sign at the end of the path, turn left and head along the pavement by the road back into Howden.

Grewelthorpe and Hackfall

Pausing on the path from Hackfall Woods to the road, with views towards Masham behind.

Located in Nidderdale, an Area of Outstanding Natural Beauty, this pretty walk starts in the charming village of Grewelthorpe. The route takes in the historic Hackfall Woods, in the care of the Woodland Trust, situated by the river Ure. There are several short climbs, and plenty of opportunities for well-behaved dogs to be let off the lead and to enjoy a paddle on this peaceful and varied walk.

Grewelthorpe is very proud of its attractive duck pond and its many resident ducks. On the edge of the village is Hackfall, a Grade I Garden in the English Heritage Register of Historic Parks and Gardens. Hackfall looks like a natural wood, but the landscape we see today is largely the result of design and work undertaken by the Aislabies of Studley Royal. In Victorian times, Hackfall was a very popular attraction and today short and medium-length walks can still be taken through the woods to discover surprise views, waterfalls, a fountain and several follies.

Dog factors

Distance: 6 miles
Road walking: A small amount leaving and returning to Grewelthorpe.
Livestock: Possibility of sheep and cattle.
Stiles: Six stiles – with varying levels of difficulty to cross.
Nearest vets: Yoredale Vets, Masham (Ripon).

Terrain
Mostly on green or woodland paths, with some short climbs.

Where to park
Street parking in Grewelthorpe (GR SE231761). **Map:** OS Explorer 298 Nidderdale

How to get there
From Ripon take the A6108 Masham road to a junction just past the village of North Stainley. Then follow the signs through Mickley to Grewelthorpe. Ripon is easily reached by the A61 from Harrogate, Thirsk or the A1.

Nearest refreshments
The Crown Inn at Grewelthorpe is dog-friendly. ☎ 01765 658210.

The Walk

1 Set off along **Lake Terrace** and head towards the edge of the village with the duck pond to the right. Just before leaving the village, turn left through a metal gate at a footpath sign next to a dog-waste bin, and head along a green enclosed track. Keep ahead on the track, ignoring gates on either side. Just before reaching a gate across the end of the track, climb a waymarked wooden stile in the hedgerow on the right – some dogs will need a helping hand, while others will go straight under it.

2 Once on the other side, turn left and follow the path along the edge of the field – take care there may be cattle here. Climb a waymarked stile – most dogs will have no problems with this one – and continue straight ahead on the path towards a gap in the hedge. There was once a stile here but not anymore, so continue through the opening into the next field and keep ahead on a green path towards another stile, which most dogs will easily pass through.

Continue on into the next field, sticking to the green path ahead towards a hedge with another waymarked stile – some dogs will need a hand over this one. Enter another field. This one may have crops growing in it, but there is a clear path through, towards the tree-line.

3 After passing a yellow waymarker, head towards a farm gate. Pass through it and then continue diagonally downhill, looking for a faded waymarker on a large wooden gate in the right-hand corner of the field. Pass through the gate into the next field and follow the green track to the right and then towards the trees. The track drops downhill as it bears left, passing a waymaker on a stump, heading towards a gate with another waymarker. Pass through the gate and continue slightly downhill towards the trees, before turning left onto a wide path down to a waymarked gate post.

4 Pass through the gate or over the stile next to it, and then continue to a waymarked wooden gate and a new stile which heads into the woods – most dogs will easily go under this stile. The wide path now continues through the woods and is easy to follow, thanks to the occasional waymarkers. Some sections of the woods are enclosed, while others are open but the path stays

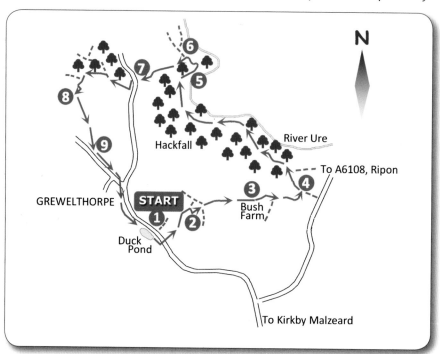

The residents of Grewelthorpe are proud of their ducks and artistically request that motorists take care near the village pond.

clear. After passing a sign for the Hackfall Woodland Trust, the **River Ure** comes into view from the right. Keep ahead, following the sign for Fisher's Hall and ignoring the path (up the steps) to Mowbray Castle. As the path narrows and becomes rocky above the river below, duckboards are provided and the way is partially blocked with boulders at one point. Cross a stream using the stepping stones and, ignoring a path up some steps to 'Garden Features', follow the yellow waymarker ahead, as the path heads slightly uphill. The river is still there to the right, and there are some pleasant views to be had.

5 Keep following the waymarkers as the path undulates before dropping closer to the water level as the trees begin to thin out. There is a beach-like area by the river, which could be a great place for your dog to have a paddle. At a fork, take the left-hand path following the waymarker towards the viewpoint. Continue uphill, winding round to the top where there is a wooden seat – perfect for a well-deserved rest while taking in the views of the river and Masham in the distance.

6 Continue on the route downhill as it re-joins the alternative path along the river shore. Just before a wooden kissing-gate by a drystone wall, turn left and follow the path uphill towards a car park. Pass through a new wooden kissing-gate into a field and continue straight ahead on a wide, green path. As the path climbs steadily, it follows a wire-and-post fence to the right, towards a new wooden gate. Pass through the kissing-gate onto an enclosed track, with a fence on one side and trees and bushes on the other. Go through another gate next to a stile near a car park, onto a quiet road.

7 Cross the road and turn left for a short distance, before turning right following a footpath sign on to a track through the trees, in to the **Swinton Estate Woodlands**. The track is wide and easy to follow with a drystone wall to the left. Just before the track starts to climb uphill, follow a path on the left as it climbs steeply before quickly levelling out, heading towards the trees ahead. Just inside the tree-line, turn left and head downhill along a path towards a small gate. Pass through it and enter the field, following the path uphill. Once at the top of the rise, turn left and head for the corner of the field where there is a broken waymarked stile – which no dogs will have a problem with. Cross the stile into the field and continue straight ahead, with the hedge to the left.

8 After a short while, cross a waymarked stile on the left – which most dogs will need help to get over, and head into another field, following the green diagonal path towards the telegraph poles. Make for another waymarked stile in the hedge ahead – some dogs will need help here, and keep going diagonally across the next field towards the trees. After crossing a broken stile – all dogs will pass through this one, enter another field and head diagonally to the right, towards a gap in the drystone wall in the far corner of the field.

9 Pass through the gap and turn left on to a road. Head back into **Grewelthorpe**, initially using the wide grass verge next to the single track road. At the junction, follow the sign for Ripon up the hill and back towards the duck pond. There is a dog-waste bin opposite the church, and another by the duck pond.

The River Ure at Lower Dunsforth

Izzy in full flight along the lush, green path back towards Lower Dunsforth at the end of the walk.

This is a very pretty riverside walk, where your dog can easily have a paddle or a swim if conditions allow. Once over the stiles at the beginning of this circular route, you and your dog can enjoy the green paths, views of the river Ure, and the wide open spaces that the Vale of York is known for. The countryside undulates gently, so if you're not up for lots of energetic climbing, then this walk is perfect. You may notice that many older properties in Lower Dunsforth still bear their 'farm' name, as until the middle of the 20th century, everyone who lived in the area was employed on the land. Today, many of the smaller farms are no longer in operation.

Dog factors

Distance: 5 miles.
Road walking: A tiny amount at the start and finish.
Livestock: Potential for sheep and cattle; please respect the signs asking for dogs to be on the lead.
Stiles: Dogs will need help to get over three stiles at the start, but the later ones all have dog-gates.
Nearest vets: Rae, Bean & Partners, Boroughbridge.

Terrain

Mostly on wide, level, grassy paths or along the embankment by the river Ure.

Where to park

By the roadside in Lower Dunsforth (GR SE439648). **Map:** OS Explorer 299 Ripon and Boroughbridge.

How to get there

Lower Dunsforth is signposted from the B6265 heading south from Boroughbridge or north from Green Hammerton on the A59 York to Harrogate road.

Nearest refreshments

The Dawnay Arms at nearby Newton-on-Ouse is dog-friendly. ☎ 01347 848345.

The Walk

1 From the Lower Dunsworth Loop information board in front of the Angler Inn, head along the wide grass verge at the side of the road, with the inn to the left. After a short distance, there are two wooden footpath signs on the other side of the road. Follow the second one to cross a stile to a narrow snicket with a wooden fence to the left and a hedge to the right. Pass through a gate into a field and head diagonally towards a stile and tree in the left corner of the field.

2 Cross the stile then turn left immediately to follow the path which skirts round the fence line, past a stone wall and a farm building to the left. Keep ahead over a flood defence mound and continue towards the hedge line, then turn left along it – keeping the hedge to the right. The path bears round to the right and passes beneath a large tree before heading to another stile in the corner of the field. Cross the stile and continue straight ahead across the field to another stile. After crossing this stile, head diagonally across an overgrown field towards a stile and farm gate to the left.

Note – because of hedge growth, some of the stiles at the start of the walk may be difficult to cross. An alternative route is to follow the road out of Lower Dunsforth, and rejoin the walk at point 3.

3 Cross the stile, or go through the gate, to a quiet road, near a junction with another lane. Cross the road and head along the quiet lane with hedgerows on either side. At the farm buildings, bear right while still on the lane, then left onto what becomes a farm track.

4 Pass a large tree to the left and a public footpath sign with directions to local villages and the river to the right. Keep ahead to a short enclosed grassy path, which leads to a metal gate. Pass through the gate into a field with a line of hawthorn trees on the left. Keeping the tree-line to the left, look for a gated footbridge across a beck to the left of the trees. Before crossing the bridge, there is an opportunity to go straight ahead to the river bank where your dog may indulge in a quick paddle.

5 After crossing the bridge, turn right along a grassy track towards the **River Ure**. The path then heads along the top of the embankment – good romping

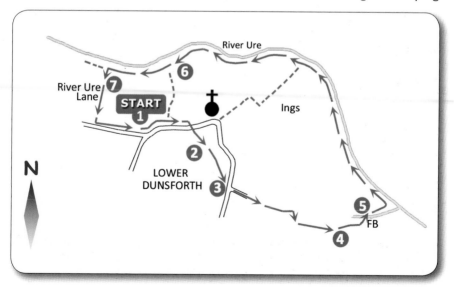

North Yorkshire - A Dog Walker's Guide

terrain for your dog when cattle and sheep are not about. Keep to the riverside path and go through numerous gates marking the boundaries of fields, while enjoying views of the river and the occasional boat. Many dogs will want to jump in the water for a quick swim.

6 Follow the path as it curves round to the north of Lower Dunsforth, from where the spire of the church is visible. The river bank becomes overgrown

The quiet, tranquil scenery by the river Ure.

near a field, with bungalows visible in the distance to the left. Cross a stile with a dog-gate into the next field, heading along a grassy path towards a large tree next to a wire-and-post fence. Continue ahead on an overgrown narrow path with a fence on each side. Cross a stile onto a similar path, and pass through three metal gates, before crossing a footbridge into a field.

7 Keep to the path by the river for a short distance before turning left to follow a waymarked path **(River Ure Lane)** across a field towards trees, a hedge line and some gates. Turn left at the gates onto the road and keep left at the junction back into **Lower Dunsforth** village.

APPENDIX

Small Animal Veterinary Practices

The following are all veterinary practices that are close to the walks described. They have been selected as handling small animals and dogs in particular.

The Beck Veterinary Practice
The Animal Health Centre, High Stakesby, Whitby YO21 1HL
☎ 01947 820333

Bishopton Veterinary Group
The Surgery, Mill Farm, Studley Road, Ripon HG4 2QR
☎ 01765 602396

Edgemoor Veterinary Practice
Station Road, Helmsley YO62 5BZ
☎ 01439 771166

Edgemoor Veterinary Practice
31a Potter Hill, Pickering YO18 8AA
☎ 01751 431380

End Cottage Veterinary Clinic
Boothferry Road, Howden DN14 7TA
☎ 01430 431758

Forest House Veterinary Surgery
29 York Place, Knaresborough HG5 0AD
☎ 01423 862121

Forrest House Veterinary Group
51 Stokesley Road, Northallerton DL6 2TS
☎ 01609 778200

The Minster Veterinary Practice
Salisbury Road, York YO26 4YN
☎ 01904 643997

Rae Bean & Partners
8 New Row, Boroughbridge, York YO51 9AX
☎ 01423 322316

Skeldale Veterinary Centre Ltd
York Road, Thirsk YO7 3BT
☎ 01845 522297

Station House Vets
Teal House, Welbury, York YO60 7EH
☎ 01653 618303

Wilton House Veterinary Clinic
Wilton Lane, Guisborough TS14 6JA
☎ 01287 637470

Yoredale Vets
Unit 1/2, Leyburn Business Park, Harmby Road DL8 5QA
☎ 01969 623024

Yoredale Vets
Masham (Ripon), The Veterinary Surgery, High Burton, Masham, Ripon HG4 4BS
☎ 01765 689422